Harro Hieronimus

Guppies, Mollies, Platys

and Other Live-bearers

Purchase, Care, Feeding, Diseases, Behavior
a Special Section on Breeding

with 23 Color Photographs
Drawings by Fritz W. Köhler

Consulting Editor: Matthew M. Vriends, Ph D

D0124910

P9-DIJ-180

BARRON'S

All inquiries should be addressed to:
Barron's Educational Series, Inc.
250 Wireless Boulevard
Hauppauge, New York 11788

Library of Congress Catalog Card No. 92-40896

International Standard Book No. 0-8120-1497-9

Library of Congress Cataloging-in-Publication Data

Hieronimus, Harro.
[Guppy, Platy, Molly und andere Lebendgebärende.
English]
Guppies, mollies, platys, and other live-bearers : purchase,
care, feeding, diseases, behavior [and] a special section on
breeding / Harro Hieronimus ; drawings by Fritz W.
Köhler ; consulting editor, Matthew M. Vriends ; [translated
from the German by Rita and Robert Kimber].
    p.   cm. -- (A Complete pet owner's manual)
Includes bibliographical references.
ISBN 0-8120-1497-9
1. Livebearing aquarium fishes.   I. Vriends, Matthew
M., 1937–   .   II. Title.   III. Series.
SF458.L58H5413   1993
639.3'753--dc20   92-40896
                                                CIP

PRINTED IN CHINA
19 18 17 16 15 14 13

The Color Photos on the Covers Show: Front cover:
Ornamental guppy variety (*Poecilia reticulata*)
Inside front cover: Ornamental guppy variety
(*Poecilia reticulata*)
Inside back cover: Sailfin molly (*Poecilia velifera*)
Back cover: Above: Ornamental guppy variety
(*Poecilia reticulata*). Below: Ornamental platy variety
(*Xiphophorus variatus*)

Photo Credits: Bitter: page 63 (below right);
Geobios/Schubert: page 46 (below, left and right);
Hartl: page 27 (above and below); Hieronimus: pages
17 (above and below, left), 18 (below), and 63 (above,
left and right; below, left); Kahl: front cover, inside
front cover; Linke: page 17 (above), inside back cover;
Nieuwenhyuzen: pages 28, 46 (above), 64 (above and
below), and back cover (above and below); Reinhard:
page 45; Werner: pages 17 (below, right) and 63
(middle).

About the Author: Harro Hieronimus is an interna-
tionally recognized aquarist, an editor for the German
Association of Live-bearing Toothed Carps, and the
author of several successful specialized books. His
principal areas of interest are breeding live-bearers
and conducting scientific research on them.

A Note of Warning: In this book, electrical equipment commonly used with aquariums is described.
Please be sure to observe the safety rules on page 16;
otherwise, there is a danger of serious accidents.

Before buying a large tank, check how much
weight the floor of your home can support in the
location where you plan to set up your aquarium (see
page 16).

Sometimes water damage occurs as a result of broken glass, overflowing, or a leak in the tank. An
insurance policy that covers such eventualities is
therefore highly recommended (see page 17).

Make sure that no one, child or adult, eats any
aquarium plants. These plants can make people sick.
Also make sure that fish medications are out of the
reach of children.

Caustic chemicals must never come into contact
with eyes, skin, or mucous membranes. In the case of
communicable fish diseases, such as fish tuberculosis, do not reach into the tank or touch the fish
with your bare hands.

Contents

Contents

Preface

Guppies, mollies, and platys are among the most popular aquarium fishes. At first glance, keeping them seems to present no problem. Every aquarium hobbyist, however, should consider these questions: Are my fish really thriving? Do they display their natural behavior and their full colors? This new Barron's pet owner's manual will help you create ideal conditions for these fish and will inform you about some interesting relatives of guppies and platys. Among these are the four-eyed fish, which can see above and below water simultaneously, and the pencil-shaped halfbeaks.

The *proper care* of these lesser known species of live-bearers requires some special knowledge on the part of the hobbyist. The author of this book, Harro Hieronimus, explains how to care for live-bearers properly and how to avoid mistakes when first setting up the tank as well as later on. Mr. Hieronimus has been keeping and breeding live-bearers for many years, and in this book he shares his practical experience. You will learn all about how these fish live in nature, that is, their natural habitats and their behavior there—information that is often useful in deciding how fish should be kept in an aquarium. And in the chapter "Advice for Buying" you will find tips on purchasing fish and on combining different species in the same tank.

Having the *right kind of tank*, setting it up correctly, and providing the appropriate water conditions are of utmost importance if you want to have a well-functioning aquarium community. Detailed information is provided on these topics, too. A separate chapter is devoted to food for the fish because a varied diet is essential to the health of live-bearers. If, in spite of excellent care and proper feeding, your fish should get sick, you can turn to the chapter "Diseases of Live-bearers" for advice and help.

If fish *reproduce successfully*, you can usually be confident that you are offering them the right conditions in the tank. There is a chapter on how to breed live-bearers and what to aim for in breeding. For many hobbyists one intriguing aspect of keeping live-bearers is that some species can be selectively bred. What this means is that, if you understand the basic laws of genetics, you can breed fish that differ in appearance from their wild ancestors in fin shape, color, and body shape. Drawing on his many years of practical experience in this area, Mr. Hieronimus offers some tips on the selective breeding of guppies, swordtails, platys, and mollies.

The last chapter of the book includes descriptions of several popular live-bearing species. For each species, you will find information on appearance, biotype, sexual differences, care and breeding, and tips on compatibility with other species.

The excellent photographs and informative drawings in the book will give you a good impression of the variety and beauty of live-bearers.

The author and the publisher wish to thank all those who have contributed to the making of this book: Ulrich Schliewen for his professional advice; the photographers for their exceptional color photos; Fritz W. Köhler for his informative drawings; and Harald Jes, director of the aquarium of the Cologne Zoo, for checking the chapter entitled "Diseases of Live-bearers."

Some Interesting Facts About Live-bearers

Introduction to a Group of Fish Families

Have you ever watched fish being born that are almost fully developed at birth? Or are you familiar with fish that can see above and below water at the same time? Keeping live-bearers, a group of fish that is becoming increasingly popular with hobbyists, gives you a chance to observe such fascinating phenomena.

For the hobbyist there are primarily four families of live-bearers that are of interest:

Live-bearing toothed carps (Poeciliidae) make up the largest group, with almost 200 species. They are called toothed carps because they have teeth on both the upper and lower jaws, though you generally need a microscope to see them.

Toothed carps are often kept in aquariums, and there is a special association for fanciers of live-bearing toothed carps (see addresses on page 70).

Mexican topminnows (Goodeidae) are not found as commonly in aquariums. About 35 species of this family of live-bearers are known.

Live-bearing halfbeaks (Hemirhamphidae) are easily distinguished from other live-bearers by their straight, pikelike bodies and their beaklike mouths. This family includes about 20 species.

Four-eyed fish (Anablepidae), the fourth family, are some of the most interesting fish you can have in an aquarium. They have the amazing faculty of seeing above and below water simultaneously.

Note: The most popular members of these four families are included in the descriptions of individual species starting on page 56, which also give instructions for care.

Where Live-bearers Come From

Live-bearers are found on only three continents: the Americas and Asia.

Live-bearing toothed carps originally all came from the Americas, their range extending from the United States in the north to Argentina in the south. Because these fish live primarily on mosquitoes and their larvae, however, scientists conceived the idea of using them to control mosquitoes biologically. Wild populations of live-bearing toothed carps, such as guppies (see page 60) and mosquito fish (*Gambusia*, see page 57), were introduced into swampy areas of Southeast Asia and the Philippines to keep in check malarial mosquitoes. From these locations the carp spread to almost all tropical and subtropical waters, including those of southern Europe.

Mexican topminnows live in the rivers and lakes of the Mexican plateau, as well as in the rivers that descend from the plateau to the Pacific Ocean.

Halfbeaks occur all over Southeast Asia. They are found from India to Indonesia and also on the Philippines. They live in both fresh and brackish water.

Birth of a Mexican topminnow. The embryos are nourished inside the mother's body through a kind of umbilical cord. The young are almost fully developed at birth.

Some Interesting Facts About Live-bearers

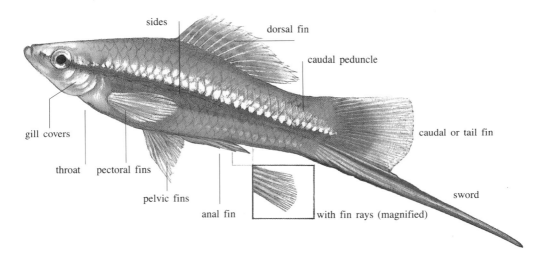

sides

dorsal fin

caudal peduncle

gill covers

caudal or tail fin

throat   pectoral fins

pelvic fins

sword

anal fin

with fin rays (magnified)

The body of a live-bearer. Familiarity with the anatomy of fish can help you identify different species.

Four-eyed fish are found along the Atlantic coasts of Central and South America (from Mexico to Brazil). Generally they live in the brackish water of mangrove swamps, but sometimes they occur in pure salt water as well. Four-eyed fish have also been discovered living in fresh water several hundred miles inland.

Live-bearers in Aquariums

European aquarists were first introduced to live-bearers around 1890. With the exciting discovery that these fish give birth to live young, live-bearers quickly became popular. Great demand resulted in very high prices. Thus German fanciers paid over 20 gold marks—more than a month's pay for a laborer—for a pair of caudos (*Phalloceros caudimaculatus*). Luckily live-bearers reproduced well in aquariums, and the prices soon dropped.

The rarer species, like members of the genus *Priapella*, were not imported until the 1960s.

Are the Latin Names Important?

Although the vernacular names of the most popular live-bearers, such as the guppy, are commonly known and used, the Latin names are still important. If you know the Latin names of your fish, you can communicate without danger of misunderstanding with aquarists from different countries. Moreover, certain species that are imported or sold more rarely have not yet acquired English names.

So-called binomial nomenclature was introduced by Carolus Linnaeus in 1758. Ever since, every organism, animal as well as plant, has been classified according to this system. The *first word* of the Latin name indicates the genus to which the

Some Interesting Facts About Live-bearers

organism belongs; the *second word*, the species. For example, the Latin name *Phalloceros caudimaculatus* tells us that this fish belongs to the genus *Phalloceros* and to the species *caudimaculatus*.

The Way of Life of Live-bearers

All hobbyists should know the natural way of life of their charges, for this information often contains clues about the proper way to keep the fish in a tank.

Social behavior: In nature, many live-bearers are shoaling fish; that is, they live in groups of at least five. In an aquarium a hierarchy generally is established within the shoal. The dominant male has more vivid colors than the other fish in the shoal and is called the alpha animal. You will observe in the aquarium that the alpha animal is always the first to eat at feeding time and drives other fish away if they get in his way. If the highest ranking male dies or is removed from the shoal, the second-ranking male, the beta animal, generally takes his place.

Most live-bearers are nonaggressive among their own species and get along with other kinds of fish as well. Only a few, like the pike live-bearer (see page 57), are predatory. They can be kept together with other fish only if the latter are about the same size.

Male swordtails are highly aggressive toward each other. Therefore, if you want to keep swordtails, it is advisable to have only one male with several females or else to have at least five males with the same or a greater number of females. In this way the aggression is "spread out" over several males and is therefore dissipated.

Tiny fry are unfortunately always in danger of being eaten if kept in the same tank with adult or juvenile live-bearers. Almost all live-bearers go after fry and will even eat their own young if they get a chance.

Courtship behavior: Courtship behavior varies a great deal among live-bearers. Many species, such as guppies and swordtails, are highly demonstrative during courtship. The male swims back and forth rapidly in front of the female, his body bending in sigmoid shape. In some other species, for example the mollies (see page 61), the male positions himself in front of the female with widely spread fins, showing off fins and colors. The purpose of all this behavior is to stimulate the female's readiness to mate.

Some other species, such as *Girardinus metallicus* (see page 58), have no such elaborate courtship displays. The male emerges suddenly from a hiding place, pounces on the female, and disappears again right after mating.

Mating: Copulation occurs the same way in all the species. The male swims alongside the female and fertilizes her with his anal fin, which serves as the copulatory organ.

The shape of the anal fin differs among species.
- In live-bearing toothed carps, the middle rays of the anal fin are modified into a copulatory organ (see drawing on page 7) when the males reach sexual maturity. The anterior and posterior rays remain noticeably smaller.

This copulatory organ is called the gonopodium. The shape of the gonopodium often helps to distinguish different genera and sometimes even species. In most species, the gonopodium ends in a more or less clearly visible hook or claw. During copulation the male briefly introduces his gonopodium into the genital opening or pore of the female. The hook or claw helps the male hold on during the transfer of the sperm packets, thereby lengthening the duration of copulation and increasing the chances of fertilization taking place. Nevertheless, often no more than one out of about ten attempts at fertilization is successful.
- The anal fin of male four-eyed fish changes into a pipe-shaped copulatory organ.
- In Mexican topminnows and in halfbeaks only the anterior part of the anal fin is somewhat

Some Interesting Facts About Live-bearers

shortened and thickened. (The *Hemirhamphodon* genus is an exception. Here only the posterior part is modified; see page 68.) The copulatory organ of these fish is called the andropodium and can be detected only if you look very closely.

Note: If the female is not interested in mating, she tries to get away from the male. For this reason you must always arrange for a few hiding places in a tank (see "Decorating Materials," page 21).

If a male pursues a female too aggressively and perhaps even injures her fins, you have to step in. Move either the female or the male to a separate tank for a few weeks, or simply increase the number of females, so that the male has more than one prospective mate to keep him busy.

Reproductive behavior: Giving birth to live young, that is, keeping and protecting the embryos inside the mother's body until they are ready for independent living, is the most highly developed form of brood care. The young of all live-bearers are born almost fully formed; only the viviparous process differs from species to species. In the family Poeciliidae, the live-bearing toothed carps, the mother carries fertilized eggs in her body, where they mature. The young emerge from the eggs shortly before they are born. With Mexican topminnows, however, the embryos are nourished in the mother's body through a kind of umbilical cord; they are not inside egg shells. The umbilical cord can still be seen for a few hours after the young are born. The embryos of four-eyed fish and some halfbeaks develop in a similar manner.

One of nature's amazing provisions is the storing of sperm in the female's body for future fertilizations. This happens in live-bearing toothed carps, four-eyed fish, and halfbeaks. During copulation the males give off more sperm packets or a greater number of sperm than are needed for fertilization at the time, and these extra sperm remain inside the female's body for use as needed. The females are thus able to have young several times after just one mating. One mosquito fish female kept in an aquarium is known to have given birth eleven times after just one mating.

Mexican topminnows have no such fertilization for multiple use. The females must be fertilized by a male again after every brood before they can have more young.

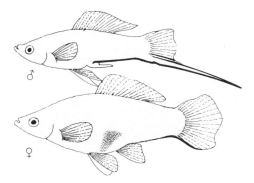

Telling the sexes apart. The male swordtail (above) has more pointed fins than the female (below). The male's anal fin has been modified into a sexual organ, the gonopodium.

Advice For Buying

Where You Can Get Live-bearers

Pet stores: Live-bearers are routinely carried by pet stores and sold at very reasonable prices, but these are usually tank-bred fish. They come from aquarium hobbyists and include all kinds of strains and colors (see page 45). Fish caught in the wild are rarely found in pet stores, mainly because the countries from which live-bearers come generally are not in the business of exporting fish. The Central American countries, for instance, are home to a great variety of live-bearing fish but do not routinely export them.

Aquarists' associations: If you would like to keep wild strains of fish, you should turn to an aquarists' society, such as the American Live-bearer Association (see "Useful Literature and Addresses," page 70). Because of the many international contacts and the travels of association members, new and interesting species are introduced almost every year. At regional and supraregional meetings, aquarists swap or sell their "treasures." (Dates and places of meetings are published in aquarists' publications; see the addresses on page 70.)

Aquarists' magazines: Breeders and members of aquarists' associations advertise routinely when they have fish to sell. Also, pet stores specializing in rarer species put ads in these magazines listing the fish they have for sale.

My Tip: I recommend strongly that buyers personally inspect any fish they consider purchasing. Checking the health of the fish yourself is the only reliable safeguard against future disappointment and unpleasant surprises.

The Best Time for Buying

It is best to buy fish in the spring, in the fall, or around Christmas. At these times the supply of live-bearers is especially large. Also, the fish have enough time to become acclimated to their new home before vacation time, so that you can leave their care to someone else (see page 29) without worrying when you go away.

Breeders generally mail fish only during the warmer season, from May to September. Dealers have special winter packaging materials and will send fish at any time of year for an extra fee.

Note: Buying fish through the mail presupposes considerable trust on the part of both the seller and the buyer. Certain qualities of the fish, such as sex and the particular strain, should always be guaranteed in writing. You should also stipulate the right to return fish that are dead on arrival. Dead fish are placed in alcohol and returned to the sender if requested.

Is This Fish Healthy?

Before buying a fish, you should take a close look at it. You can detect many diseases from an animal's external appearance. Examine particularly the body, the skin, the fins, the eyes, and the gills (see drawing, page 11).

Body: The abdomen of a healthy live-bearer always looks convex in profile, more so in females than in males. These fish have a "chubby" look. This is true even of females that have just given birth, even though the fish may actually be very slender. All other fish should appear well fed.

Watch out for fish with bloated bellies and protuberant scales! These fish are incurably sick.

A disproportionately large head is usually a sign that the fish has undergone prolonged hunger periods. This does not mean the fish will die soon, but it should probably not be used for breeding.

Skin: The skin should not show any white film, mold, or white dots (see "Diseases of Live-bearers," page 37). The scales should hug the body smoothly. Examine the tip of the mouth with special care to make sure that no white film is evident there.

Advice for Buying

Fins: Missing or only partially formed fins are always a bad sign. Frayed edges on the fins are usually the result of disease (see page 37).

In healthy fish the fins (except for the dorsal fin in some species) stick out visibly from the body. A fish that clamps its fins close to its body and perhaps rocks from side to side is not feeling well and is therefore especially susceptible to disease.

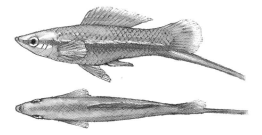

Checking the State of Health. When buying fish, look at the head closely both from above and from the side.

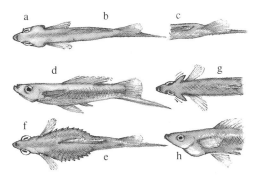

Don't buy the fish if you observe the following:
a. There is a sharp break between the head and the sides of the body.
b. The body is considerably narrower than the head.
c. There is a thickening of the caudal peduncle.
d. The fins are clamped close to the body.
e. The abdomen is bloated.
f. The eyes protrude.
g. The gill covers are permanently extended.
h. There is a swelling at the throat.

Eyes: The eyes should be clear and should never protrude unnaturally from the head.

Gills: Healthy fish breathe slowly. They breathe somewhat faster in a densely populated tank. As the fish breathe, the gill covers open slightly, and you can see the gill tissue underneath. In healthy fish it is a pale reddish color.

My Tip: Buy only fish that appear to be in good health, even if you are tempted to do otherwise because you have just found a fish you have long been looking for. Introducing sick fish has led to disaster in many tanks with previously all healthy fish.

Should You Buy Single Fish, Pairs, or a Shoal?

Many live-bearers are shoaling fish, and you should therefore always buy at least a pair or, preferably, several fish. A shoal consists of at least five or six fish, with the females outnumbering the males (for example, two males and three or four females).

In the case of swordtails (see page 65), however, the ratio should be different because the males are very aggressive toward each other. Buy a small shoal of five or six fish that includes only one male.

Buy live-bearers *singly* only if you can get a pregnant female, with whose offspring you hope to build up a strain.

My Tip: Make sure that the fish are about the same size when you buy them. Young females, in particular, can suffer if larger males pursue them, and there can also be problems at feeding time. The bigger fish often snap up the food without letting the smaller ones get at it or chase them away from the feeding place.

Telling the Sex

Telling the sexes apart is very easy, at least once the fish reach adolescence.

Males: In male live-bearing toothing carps, the anal fin becomes modified into the gonopodium (see pages 8 and 9), which is always pointed and much thinner than the anal fin of the female. The andropodium (see page 9) of Mexican topminnows and halfbeaks is often hard to distinguish and does not become apparent until the fish are almost full grown. However, the sex of these species is generally easy to identify by the colors of the fish; the males are much more brightly colored than the females. Also, the dorsal fin of the male may be larger and differently shaped (for example, somewhat elongated).

The males of all live-bearers are slimmer than the females and usually remain somewhat smaller. This difference becomes apparent, however, only when the fish are almost full grown.

Females: The females of all live-bearers have normally shaped anal fins. In almost all species the area in front of the anal fin is darker in color. This dark spot, which is particularly noticeable when the female is highly pregnant, is often called the gravid spot. Among the live-bearers, only the females of four-eyed fish and of halfbeaks lack such a spot.

Female live-bearers are generally bigger and fatter than the males.

Note: In live-bearers the ground color is the same for both sexes except in halfbeaks and Mexican topminnows.

My Tip: It is often impossible to tell the sex of fry and juvenile fish. What you have to do in this case is to get at least five fish and hope that there will be some of both sexes.

Transporting Live-bearers

How to best transport live-bearers depends on their size and on the aggressiveness of the species.

Baby fish up to ³/₄ inches (2 cm) long can be placed in groups of five or six in the plastic bags normally used for transporting fish and can stay there for some time.

Fish up to 2³/₄ inches (7 cm) long can be transported either singly in the usual plastic bags, or by pairs in larger bags.

Fish over 2³/₄ inches (7 cm) long should always be packed one to a bag.

Mexican topminnows should always be transported singly. In the confinement of the bag, these fish become aggressive. If even two fish are together, one may kill the other in a very short time.

The rule for any transportation of fish is that the bag be filled only about one-fifth with water. There should be as much air in the bag as possible to allow for air exchange. Fill the bag with a membrane pump or, if necessary, inflate it with air from your mouth.

If the fish are to travel for more than eight hours, the bag may be inflated with pure oxygen. Expecially at the height of summer, it may become very hot inside the bag. As little as 15 minutes in a car in full sun (even while driving) can be fatal for the fish. In winter, the bag will cool down equally quickly. Pet dealers often wrap the bag containing fish in newspapers. This helps protect the fish briefly against excessive temperature fluctuations and also provides darkness. The fish are less active in a darkened bag, and the stress of the journey is thus lessened somewhat.

Note: If fish are mailed, the transport bag should always be enclosed in a Styrofoam box to prevent extreme temperature fluctuations. If you mail fish yourself, do not feed them for at least one day beforehand; otherwise the transport water will become too dirty.

Is Quarantine Absolutely Necessary?

In my opinion, fish that appear healthy don't have to be quarantined. Place the newly acquired fish in the regular tank when you bring them home, even if other fish are already living in it. Some pathogens are present in any tank, and even a water change can lead to an outbreak of disease.

If, however, you want to avoid all possible risk, you can place the new fish in a separate tank. Then, after a quarantine period of three to four weeks, healthy fish can join the fish you already have in the regular tank.

Introducing the Fish

Proceed with caution when you transfer the fish into the tank. First let the bag with the new fish in it float for about 20 minutes in the tank where they are going to live. Then, using water from the tank, add to the bag about half again as much water as it originally contained. Pin the top of the bag under the tank cover, so that the bag floats on the water surface, and wait another 20 minutes. Then you can let the fish swim out of the bag into the tank.

Species Tank or Community Tank?

As the names suggest, a species tank contains only one kind of fish, such as mosquito fish, whereas in a community tank several different but compatible species are combined. A community can consist of different kinds of live-bearers, or it may include other suitable fish (see page 14).

Species tank: Only a very few live-bearers require a species tank (see "Popular Live-bearers and Their Care," page 56). Having a tank to themselves is especially important for small, sensitive species, such as *Poecilia brannerie* , as well as for very large ones, such as pike live-bearers (*Belonesox*).

If you plan to do selective breeding (see "Breeding Live-bearers," page 41), a species tank is obviously useful because you have to be able to

watch the fish to be bred carefully and to check on them at any time.

Community tank: Most live-bearers display their natural behavior and feel comfortable in a community tank. Some species can even be bred in a community tank (see instructions for care, beginning on page 56).

Tips on Combining Species

When you choose the fish for a community tank, there are a few general rules you should observe. Special requirements of individual species are mentioned in the instructions for care starting on page 56.

Size of fish: Combine only fish that are about the same size. Small fish that live with larger ones are clearly under constant stress. The bigger ones often assert their superior strength at the feeding place and don't let the smaller ones eat in peace. This is true not just of live-bearers but of almost all fish that live in a community.

Behavior: Quiet (what we might call "shy") fish that like to hide should not be combined with very active ones. Combine only fish with similar behavior; that is, place only species that don't disturb each other in the various regions of a community tank. Peaceful fish generally cannot hold their own against rougher species. There are some species of live-bearers, such as the guppy, in which the male follows the female around almost constantly, performing courtship displays. If not enough females are present, the males follow other fish and bother them with their sexual overtures. Fast swimmers can easily get away, but slower ones suffer from these constant pursuits.

Regional preferences: When you plan the population of a community tank, you should always make sure that the different areas of the tank will be occupied with about equal density. Many live-bearers prefer the middle stratum, and some like the top. Except for a few rarely kept species of

Advice for Buying

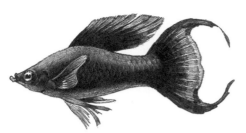

Ornamental variety of the molly. The most famous selectively bred variety is the black molly. Both its body and its fins are black.

Mexican topminnows, hardly any live-bearers live close to the bottom.

It is therefore a good idea to combine live-bearers that prefer different areas of the tank. Live-bearers and bottom dwellers like catfishes are a particularly good match. (See below, "What Fish Are Compatible?")

My Tip: You should watch the behavior of the fish in your aquarium regularly. If you notice that a fish is being picked on by another, remove either the victim or the aggressor.

Environmental conditions in nature: In the case of most live-bearers you don't have to pay too much attention to the environmental conditions that prevail in their native habitats. These fish can adjust to almost any conditions you may offer in the tank because most fish you are likely to buy are tank-bred rather than caught in the wild. Most live-bearers are comfortable in temperatures between 75 and 81°F (24 and 27°C). Many Goodeidae species from the central plateau of Mexico, however, originally come from water quite a bit cooler than the temperatures we generally maintain in our tanks, and this factor has to be taken into consideration (see "Popular Live-bearers and Their Care, page 56). Also, some live-bearers, such as *Poecilia velifera*, have adapted to brackish water. Salt must be added to the tank water (see page 61) if these fish are to thrive.

Fish with unusual requirements can be kept in a community tank, but the community must be composed of fish with similar preferences or needs.

What Fish Are Compatible?

Many live-bearers can easily be combined with other kinds of fish of the right sort. Some compatible species are listed below.

American Characins

Genera: *Hyphessobrycon*, *Hemigrammus*. Way of life: Shoal fish (at least six). For tanks holding 15 gallons (60 L) or more. Food: Live, frozen, and dry. Water: 4–25°dH, pH 6.7–7.5, 73–81°F (23–27°C). Companion fish for: Guppies, platys, mollies, medium-sized *Poecilia* species, *Priapella*, *Phallichthys*.

Armored Catfishes

Genera: *Aspidoras*, *Brochis*, *Corydoras*. Way of life: Shoal fish. For tanks holding 15 gallons (60 L) or more. Food: Omnivorous fish that generally feed on the bottom. Water: 4–20°dH, pH 6.7–7.5, 72–79°F (22–26°C). Companion fish for: All live-bearers.

Other Kinds of Catfish

Families: Loricariidae (sucker-mouth armored catfishes), all species that do not grow too large; Mochocidae (upside-down catfishes), small species. Way of life: Fish live singly or in pairs in hiding places on the bottom and form territories there. For tanks holding 20 gallons (80 L) or more. Food: Omnivorous fish; some, such as *Ancistrus*, also clean up algae. Water: 4–25°dH, pH 6.7–7.5, 68–79°F (20–26°C), though for many species the temperature can be as high as 86°F (30°C). Companion fish for: All live-bearers.

Advice for Buying

Small Cichlids

Genera: *Apistogramma*, *Microgeophagus*, *Laetacara*, *Nannacara*, small "*Cichlasoma*," West African dwarf cichlids. Way of life: Keep in pairs; fish are territorial and aggressive in the bottom area. For tanks holding 25 gallons (100 L) or more. For smaller tanks holding at least 15 gallons (60 L), choose smaller species. Food: Primarily frozen and live. Water: 4–20°dH, pH 6.7–7.5, 73–82°F (23–28°C). Companion fish for: Medium-sized and large live-bearers; can be kept in shoals in sufficiently large tanks.

My Tip: Many cichlids that are normally shy and live hidden from sight will emerge from hiding much more often if there are a few live-bearers in the tank.

Barbs and Rasboras

Genera: *Brachydanio*, *Barbus*, *Rasbora*. Way of life: Shoal fish (at least six). For tanks holding 15 gallons (60 L) or more. Food: Omnivorous fish. Water: 5–25°dH, pH 6.7–7.5, 70–81°F (21–27°C). Companion fish for: Small and medium-sized live-bearers that match them in size.

Labyrinth Fish

Genera: *Betta*, *Colisa*, *Trichogaster*. Way of life: Solitary (fighting fish, *Betta splendens*) or living in pairs. For tanks holding 20 gallons (80 L) or more. Food: Omnivorous fish. Water: 5–25°dH, pH 6.7–7.5, 72–86°F (22–30°C). Companion fish for: All medium-sized and large live-bearers (except predatory ones).

Maintenance and Care

If you want to keep live-bearers that are happy and healthy and that you can breed, you will have to supply optimal living conditions. To do so, you will need a tank of adequate size, set up and planted appropriately for the species in question, and some technical equipment, such as a filter, a heater, and artificial lighting.

Safety Precautions

Aquarium filters, heaters, and lights work on electricity. Everyone knows that the combination of electricity and water spells danger (see "A Note of Warning," page 2). Be sure, therefore, to observe the following safety rules:
- When you buy electrical equipment, be sure it is Underwriters Laboratory (UL) approved.
- Check that any electrical equipment to be operated in the tank carries a label saying that it is designed for such use.
- Buy an electronic safety device (available in aquarium stores or from electricians' suppliers) that will immediately cut off the current in case of malfunctioning apparatus or a faulty wire.
- Unplug all electric wires before you handle anything in the water or remove electrical equipment from the tank.
- If something needs to be repaired, don't try to fix it yourself; call in a licensed electrician.

The Right Aquarium

Material: I recommend a glass tank caulked with black silicone rubber. The black rubber keeps light from penetrating and thus prevents algae from growing beneath the material and causing leaks.

Plastic tanks scratch easily, and for this reason I use them only for keeping some small species and for rearing fry during the first few days of life.

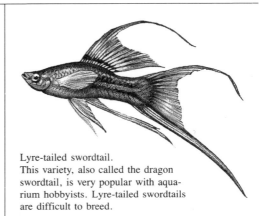

Lyre-tailed swordtail.
This variety, also called the dragon swordtail, is very popular with aquarium hobbyists. Lyre-tailed swordtails are difficult to breed.

Important: Be sure, if you want to buy a large aquarium, to consider the weight of the filled tank (see page 2). One quart (1 L) of water weighs about 2.2 pounds (1 kg). Therefore, an aquarium measuring 40 × 16 × 16 (100 × 40 × 40 cm) may easily weigh up to 440 pounds (200 kg) if heavy decorations are included. If you live in an older building or on an upper floor, you should try to find out the weight-bearing capacity of your floors (ask your landlord or an architect).

Size and capacity: The bigger the fish you would like to keep, the larger the tank should be. A good rule of thumb is that the long side of the tank should be about ten times the length of the largest full-grown fish to be kept in the tank.

Fish in a crowded tank are not happy. Keep this fact in mind when deciding on the capacity of the tank. Here is another handy rule of thumb: At least 1 liter of water is required per centimeter of fish length (adult size). One liter is equal to just over 1 quart, and one centimeter is equivalent to $^3/_8$ inch.

Live-bearing toothed carps. Above: The golden molly (*Poecilia sphenops*), a new ornamental variety. Below, left: Male molly of a wild strain (*Poecilia butleri*). Below, right: Porthole live-bearer (*Poeciliopsis gracilis*).

Maintenance and Care

Keep capacity in mind, too, when you purchase juvenile fish! Your aquarium dealer can tell you the capacity of a tank, or you can calculate it yourself by multiplying height, length, and depth and then dividing by 1,000. This calculation is a lot easier if you use the metric system. For example, 30 cm (height) × 60 cm (length) × 33 cm (depth) = 59,400 cm³. Divide by 1,000, and you get 59.4 liters. From this you will have to subtract at least 15 percent for decorations and some space above the water. In this example, you will therefore end up with about 50 liters, which is equivalent to 12½ gallons.

Important: The nightmare of many aquarists, namely, that the tank will burst, turns into reality only infrequently, but one should still be prepared for such an eventuality. Water damage—which can also be caused by overflowing or leakage—is usually very expensive to repair. For this reason you should make arrangements before you buy your aquarium to have water damage included in your home owner's or property insurance policy. Ask your insurance agent what costs are covered in case of an accident.

Cover: Since many live-bearers are excellent jumpers, you should have a tightly fitting cover for your tank. Especially for smaller tanks, covers with aquarium lights installed in them are practical. If you have lights that hang above the tank, place a glass cover over the tank.

Location: The aquarium should not stand next to a window; otherwise, too many algae may form. You can afford not to worry about this only if you have live-bearers such as mollies (see page 61) that consume massive amounts of algae.

Live-bearing toothed carps. Above: Ornamental swordtail variety (*Xiphophorus helleri*) with fins of normal length. Below: Blue-eyed live-bearers (*Priapella intermedia*).

Heating

Except for Mexican topminnows (see page 66), almost all live-bearers are not really comfortable unless they are kept at a temperature of at least 72°F (22°C). This means that you need a heater to raise the water temperature and a thermometer to check it.

Thermostatically controlled heaters are my recommendation. The heater will be appropriate for the size of your tank if the number of watts is about half as large as the number of quarts of water in the tank. For example, if you have a 15-gallon or 60-quart (60-L) tank, you will need a heater with a capacity of about 30 watts.

My Tip: In order for the heat to spread evenly throughout the tank, it is best to place the heater near the filter outflow or the water circulator.

Heating elements can be installed outside the tank. The water is heated in them, and an outside filter acts as pump. You can also buy outside filters with built-in heating elements (thermofilters).

Filtration

A filter is essential for maintaining stable water conditions in the aquarium. Potentially toxic substances, such as leftover food, excreta, and decaying parts of plants, are sucked up and broken down biologically in the filter. The "clean" water that flows back also supplies fresh oxygen. However, filters are no substitute for water changes at regular intervals (see page 24).

Air-driven inside filters are especially useful for rearing tanks and small aquariums holding up to 12½ gallons (50 L). A membrane pump sucks the water across filter wadding or foam. In plastic inside filters, crushed lava or porous ceramic filter material can also be used.

My Tip: Bacteria that fulfill an important biological role establish themselves in the filter material. You should therefore never replace all the filter material; just rinse some of it under lukewarm water and then return it to the filter.

Maintenance and Care

Motorized inside filters should be a suitable size for the tank in which they are used. They should circulate all the water in the tank about three times per hour. These filters work well for tanks holding between 12½ and 50 gallons (50 and 200 L).

Outside filters come in two versions. One type is hung on the tank wall from the outside and operates without hoses. Much more common and more practical are the canister filters. They are placed outside the aquarium (behind it, for instance, or in a cupboard underneath the tank) and connected to it by means of hoses. The canister is large enough to accommodate several different filter materials. The filtering capacity should be about twice the tank content. A canister filter doesn't need cleaning until the flow through it is noticeably slowed down. Outside filters are cleaned the same way as inside filters.

My Tip: Install a small filter with wadding inside the tank. It will remove the worst dirt from the water before it reaches the main filter, thereby avoiding the need for many cleanings of the main filter.

Ideal filter materials are all filter wadding and other materials with large surface areas, such as porous filtering ceramics or balls of artificial material manufactured for this express purpose. I place a thick layer of coarse filter wadding at the bottom of each of my canister filters and replace it when I clean the filter. On top of that I put filtering ceramic material, which is topped with wadding, but of a finer consistency. The ceramic material and the fine wadding I merely rinse with lukewarm water when I clean the unit.

Peat should not be used as a filter material for live-bearers. Most of these fish don't like the substances contained in peat. Also, peat acidifies the water to quite an extent, and most species don't do well in water with a low pH (see page 23).

Important: Don't try to use the cotton wool sold for household purposes. It is totally unsuitable for use in a filter because it doesn't allow the water to flow through it freely. Always buy your filter wadding at an aquarium or pet store.

Lighting

Tanks in which live-bearers are kept may be lit brightly. Light does encourage algae growth, but most live-bearers like to eat algae along with other food. If there is no nutrient excess in the tank water (caused by too many fish or too lavish feeding) and the tank is not too near a window, no undesirable (blue) algae will form. Only green algae, which are fit food for many live-bearers, will be present.

The period of artificial lighting is best regulated with an automatic timer. The lights should be on 10 to 14 hours a day.

Incandescent light bulbs should be used only for small rearing tanks. They cause excessive algae growth.

Fluorescent lights are suitable for all tanks 12 to 20 inches (30 to 50 cm) deep. Most aquariums come with covers that have fittings for mounting flourescent tubes in them. Quite a variety of shades of fluorescent light is available. I use warm-tone lights if the cover accommodates only one fluorescent tube. If there is room for more than one tube, I combine warm-tone and Growlux (red-tone) tubes. The Growlux tubes not only enhance plant growth but also make the color of the fish (especially red ones) show up more brilliantly. Hard white lights stimulate algae growth. In recent years fluorescent tubes that give off an especially bright light have become available. They, too, are highly suitable and have two advantages: they use less electricity, and they last longer. These qualities more than compensate for their higher price.

Normal fluorescent tubes age quickly, and as they do their light output decreases. If you care about having thriving plants, you should replace these tubes annually. If there are several tubes, change one at a time because plants are sometimes sensitive to drastic changes in light conditions. For the same reason you should also avoid changing from one light tone to another.

Maintenance and Care

Mercury vapor lamps (HQL) and halogen vapor lamps (HQI) are recommended for aquariums deeper than 20 inches (50 cm). They give off a great quantity of light. One lamp is sufficient for a tank about 30 inches (75 cm) long; a 5-foot (150-cm) tank would thus require two of these lamps. The HQI lamps put out even more light than the HQL ones and can thus be used for tanks 24 or more inches (60 cm) deep.

My Tip: For large aquariums, HQL or HQI lamps often turn out to be less expensive than the combined cost of fluorescent lights and the cover in which they are installed. They also last longer than fluorescent lights.

Important: Because of the mercury contained in HQL and HQI lamps, the burnt-out units may not be thrown away with ordinary household trash but must be disposed of as hazardous waste.

Bottom Material

The bottom of the water in most natural habitats where live-bearers are found is light in color. Consequently almost all of these fish display their natural behavior and their lovely colors to best advantage in an aquarium with light bottom material. Red shades, however, show up better above dark bottom material. As far as I can tell, live-bearers seem just as content in a tank with dark bottom material as in one with a light bottom.

River sand or gravel, available at aquarium stores in different grades ranging from 0.08 to 0.2 inch (2 to 5 mm), makes a good bottom material.

My Tip: Don't use more than 20 percent sand in the mixture for the bottom. Pure sand quickly packs solid and promotes organic decay.

Important: Gravel and sand should be rinsed until the rinse water runs clear before they are put into the tank. Even so, the water in the tank may get slightly cloudy, but this does not harm the fish and the water will clear up in a day or two with effective filtering.

Crushed basalt and lava, because of their dark color, set off the reddish shades of fish particularly well. Use only basalt and lava with rounded edges, however, so that bottom-dwelling fish you may want to introduce into the aquarium will not get hurt.

My Tip: I have had very good success using a mixture of 60 percent gravel ranging from 0.08 to 0.2 inch (2 to 5 mm) in diameter, 30 percent crushed basalt or lava with rounded edges, and 10 percent sand as bottom material.

Planting

An aquarium without plants looks empty and barren. But plants are not only visually attractive; they also fulfill an important role in maintaining water quality because they produce oxygen. Dense plant growth also provides needed hiding places for the fish. You will find the most important aquarium plants, along with instructions for their care, listed on pages 25 and 26. The terms used under the heading "Light" mean the following: dim = 0.3 watt per quart of water; medium = 0.45 watt per quart of water; bright = 0.6 watt per quart of water. For example, if you want to illuminate the plants in a 25-gallon tank brightly, you will need 60 watts ($100 \times 0.6 = 60$). You can use either a 60-watt mercury vapor lamp or two 30-watt neon tubes.

My Tip: Don't skimp on plants. Plant the tank generously when you first set it up.

Decorating Materials

To supply hiding places for weaker fish as well as for fry, you can use not only plants but also other items available at aquarium stores. With these you can create underwater landscapes.

Pine or oak roots from bogs, where they have lain airtight for centuries, are suitable. These roots become waterlogged and stay on the bottom. Never use other types of roots because they may rot. Roots from bogs do, however, acidify the tank water considerably and should therefore be used only sparingly.

My Tip: Boil small roots before placing them in the aquarium. They quickly absorb water. Weigh larger roots down with rocks.

Rocks, such as granite and slate slabs (available at aquarium stores), can be grouped to form structures. However, do not lay the rocks directly on the bottom because they may crack the glass. You can either cover the bottom side of the lowermost rocks with a layer of silicone rubber be-

fore putting them on the aquarium bottom, or press them into the bottom material. Since most livebearers don't mind hard water, the rocks don't have to be limefree.

Important: Glue together largish rock structures with silicone glue to make sure the rocks will not slide against the glass.

Clay flower pots are readily used by the fish to hide in. Before placing the pot upside down on the bottom material, break a piece out of the edge of the pot to form an entrance.

The Ten Steps in Setting Up an Aquarium

1. Rinse the tank with cold water.

2. Place the washed bottom material in the tank. Spread it in such a way that it is about twice as high in the back as in the front; the aquarium will look more attractive that way. In order for the plants to become well rooted, the bottom material should be at least 2 inches (5 cm) deep.

3. Carefully fill the tank about one-third full with water that is at room temperature. When doing this, set a saucer on the bottom material and aim the water at the saucer, so that the bottom material doesn't get stirred up too much.

4. Place the decorating materials in the tank.

5. Plant the aquarium. Large plants should go in the back; small ones, toward the front.

6. Place a sheet of newspaper on top of the water, and carefull fill the tank the rest of the way, up to about 1½ inches (4 cm) from the top.

7. Now install the heater and the filter. Make sure that the filter intake and outflow are as far apart as possible.

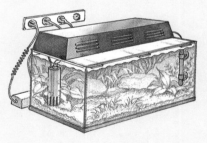

An aquarium set up and ready for use. You should run a newly set up aquarium for about two weeks without fish in it.

8. Cover the aquarium and set up the lights (if they are not part of the cover). Since many live-bearers like to jump, fill in any cracks between tank and cover with foam rubber.

9. Turn on the filter, heater, and lights.

10. Be sure to check the temperature and pH before you introduce the fish.

Maintenance and Care

The Right Aquarium Water

The aquarist has to be familiar with the requirements of his charges if the fish and plants in the aquarium are to thrive. The crucial factors are water hardness and the pH value or degree of acidity or alkalinity of the water.

Water Hardness

Total water hardness is expressed in degrees dH, and water is usually classified as follows:
0 to 4°dH = very soft
5 to 8°dH = soft
9 to 12°dH = medium hard
13 to 20°dH = hard
21°dH and up = very hard

In nature almost all live-bearers live in medium hard or hard water. Consequently many live-bearers are not happy in soft water, especially if it has a low pH (see below), and fail to thrive under such conditions.

Measuring water hardness: Both total and carbonate hardness must be measured. Aquarium stores sell kits that indicate both types of hardness and are easy to use. You don't need to measure the hardness more than once a week.

The correct water hardness for live-bearers: Total hardness should be above 7°dH for both the regular maintenance and the breeding of live-bearers. Fish that live in brackish water are an exception to this rule. In the descriptions of popular live-bearers starting on page 56 you will find exact information on the ideal water conditions for each species.

My Tip: Quite often, regular tap water will be adequate for use in a tank with live-bearers. To find out the hardness of your tap water, all you have to do is call or write to your local water company.

pH Value

The pH value indicates the degree of acidity or alkalinity of the water. A pH of 7 means that the water is neutral. Water with a pH below 7 is considered acidic; a pH above 7 indicates alkaline water. Since the pH scale is logarithmic, water with a pH of 6 has ten times as many acidic particles as water with a pH of 7.

Measuring the pH: The simplest way is to use a liquid indicator sold at aquarium stores. There are also indicator sticks, available from dealers in chemicals. If you need to measure the pH several times in a row, electronic measuring instruments are very useful and, in the long run, cheaper.

The correct pH for live-bearers: This value is between 6.5 and 8. Again, fish from brackish water are an exception (see the instructions for care beginning on page 56). For these species, the pH may be as high as 8.5.

Changing the pH: Aquarium dealers sell useful kits for both raising and lowering the pH. Every time you do something to change the water properties, be sure to measure the pH immediately afterward.

Nitrite and Nitrate

Aquarium water is bound to contain many organic waste products, produced by fish excreta, excess food, and decaying animal and plant matter. In the breakdown of these materials, nitrite, which is toxic for fish, is formed. Bacteria in the bottom material, in the filter, and in the water transform nitrite into less harmful nitrate, but this transformation process uses up oxygen. Aquarium plants, however, produce oxygen, and you can avoid excess nitrite concentrations by having plenty of plants in the tank and—especially important—by refraining from keeping too many fish in one tank.

High nitrite concentrations: These are often found in newly set-up tanks. You can tell that the nitrite concentration is excessive if the fish are panting. If this occurs, immediately change one-third of the water (see below). To avoid a buildup of nitrites in a new tank, let the tank sit with the filter running for two weeks before introducing the fish.

Measuring nitrite and nitrate content: Aquarium dealers sell kits for this purpose that are easy to use.

Changing the Water

The more fish that live in a tank, the more important it is to change the water regularly. With-out water changes, the mortality rate of the fish rises, and they will fail to reproduce.

When changing the water, replace no more than one-third at a time if the new water is of the same temperature as the tank water, and no more than one-fifth if the new water is cooler. If you change the water every four to six weeks, you will have nothing to worry about. If the tank is crowded or if you feed the fish more lavishly than normal—as when raising young fish—you will need to change the water more frequently (see Maintenance Schedule, below).

Maintenance Schedule

Daily	Weekly	Monthly	Every three months	Annually
• Feed.	• Thin plants that have become too dense.	• Change water.	• Clean filter thoroughly.	• Clean tank thoroughly, removing and rinsing bottom material.
• Check heater, temperature, and filtration/ circulation.	• Replace water that has evaporated.	• Siphon off detritus.	• Check electric wires for possible damage.	• Replace fluorescent light tubes.
• Remove dead fish, if any, and dead plant parts.	• Check pH.	• Remove algae.	• Check air and filter hoses.	
• Observe behavior of fish.		• Tend plants (see page 26).		

Swordtail. Berlin cross-breed.

Aquarium Plants

Anubias barteri var. *nana*
Distribution: Tropical and subtropical West Africa.
Care: Set in substrate, or tie to roots or rocks.
Light: Dim to bright.
Water: 2–20°dH, 68–86°F (20–30°C), pH 6–8.
Propagation: Side shoots on the roots (rhizomes).
Location: Foreground of tank.

Hornwort

Ceratophyllum demersum
Distribution: Worldwide.
Care: Do not set in ground; floats unattached in water; fast growing.
Light: Bright to very bright.
Water: 5–25°dH, 59–77°F (15–25°C), pH 6–8; also, slightly brackish water.
Propagation: Side shoots.
Location: Upper third of tank.

Water fern or water sprite

Ceratopteris thalictroides
Distribution: Tropical areas in the Americas, Asia, Africa, and northern Australia.
Care: Can be planted in substrate or left floating.
Light: Dim if free floating; otherwise bright to very bright.
Water: 5–20°dH, 68–86°F (20–30°C), pH 6–7.5.
Propagation: Adventitious plants at tips of leaves.
Location: Back or middle of tank (set in substrate); upper third of tank.

Cryptocoryne wendtii
Distribution: Sri Lanka.
Care: Sensitive to sudden, drastic changes in water properties; no other problems.
Light: Dim to bright.
Water: 5–20°dH, 68–86°F (20–30°C), pH 6–8.
Propagation: Numerous runners.
Location: Middle or background of tank.

Slender-leaved Amazon

Echinodorus amazonicus
Distribution: Brazil.
Care: Needs frequent water changes; keep water clear.
Light: Bright to very bright.
Water: 2–15°dH, 72–82°F (22–28°C), pH 6.5–7.5.
Propagation: Adventitious plants on submerged flower stems.
Location: Plant singly in back of tank.

Pygmy chain

Echinodorus tenellus
Distribution: Brazil to United States.
Care: Supply plenty of fresh water.
Light: Bright.
Water: 2–15°dH, 68–86°F (20–30°C), pH 6–7.5.
Propagation: Runners.
Location: Foreground of tank.

Moneywort or creeping Jenny

Lysimachia nummularia
Distribution: Europe, Japan, western United States.
Care: Plant in small clusters.
Light: Bright to very bright; not a floating plant.
Water: 5–20°dH, 59–75 °F (15–24°C), pH 6–8.
Propagation: Cuttings from side shoots.
Location: Middle or background of tank.

Swordfern

Microsorium pteropus
Distribution: Tropical Southeast Asia.
Care: Tie to rocks or roots, or weigh rhizome down. Do not set in substrate.
Light: Very dim to bright.
Water: 2–20°dH, 68–86°F (20–30°C), pH 5.5–8.
Propagation: Adventitious plants on rhizomes and tips of leaves.
Location: Middle or background of tank.

Najas indica
Distribution: Tropical Asia.
Care: Can be set in substrate or left floating below the water surface.
Light: Bright to very bright.
Water: 2–20°dH, 64–86°F (18–30°C), pH 6–8.
Propagation: Shoots in axils.
Location: Middle or upper third of tank.

Dwarf arrowhead or needle sagittaria

Sagittaria subulata var. *pusilla*
Distribution: Eastern North America.
Care: Plant in small clusters.
Light: Bright to very bright.
Water: 2–20°dH, 68–86°F (20–30°C), pH 6–8.
Propagation: Runners.
Location: Middle or background of tank.

Corkscrew vallisneria

Vallisneria spiralis
Distribution: Tropics and subtropics.
Care: Best planted in small clusters.
Light: Bright to very bright.
Water: 5–20°dH, 59–86°F (15–30°C), pH 6–8.
Propagation: Runners.
Location: Back of tank.

Java moss

Vesicularia dubyana
Distribution: India, extending to Malay Peninsula.
Care: Tie to rocks or roots, or let float free.
Light: Dim to bright.
Water: 2–20°dH, 64– 86°F (18–30°C), pH 5.5–7.5.
Propagation: Vigorous production of shoots.
Location: Middle or foreground of tank.

Live-bearing halfbeaks. Above: Wrestling or Malayan halfbeak (*Dermogenys pusillus*). Below: *Nomorhamphus liemi liemi*.

Maintenance and Care

When You Go Away...

When you go away, it is best if someone knowledgeable about fish and aquariums can step in for you. Measure out the food portions in advance, place each portion in a small envelope, and write on it the date when it is to be used. Also prepare a schedule of when the most important chores and checkings need to be performed.

Aquarium Plants

Your dream of lush and healthy aquarium plants can easily become reality if you plant them properly, offer them the conditions they need to thrive (see descriptions of plants, pages 25 and 26), and tend to them regularly.

Planting: Wash visible dirt particles and snails, if there are any, off the plants under running, lukewarm water. Remove wilted leaves and expose the roots. With a very sharp knife trim the roots to about 2 to 2½ inches (5 to 6 cm). Roots should also be cut when plants are moved and when the bottom material gets its thorough cleaning. When you set the plants into the aquarium, make sure the roots are not at an angle but point as straight down as possible into the bottom material.

Important: Aquarium plants are often sold in pots with mineral wool, and stem plants are sometimes weighted down with a lead ribbon. Wash the roots of such plants especially thoroughly. Mineral wool and lead ribbons should under no circumstances end up in the aquarium.

Live-bearing toothed carps. The "tuxedo" variety of the sunset platy (*Xiphophorus variatus*) has an especially striking black area on its sides.

Ensuring good plant growth: Plants need three things to grow well: adequate light, good water quality, and nutrients. Of these, light is surely the most crucial factor for aquarium plants. Most of them require a great deal of light (see plant descriptions on pages 25 and 26). Too dense a layer of floating plants shuts out most of the light from above, so that many bottom plants will not grow properly. In that case, you have to thin the floating plants (see "Plant Care," below). Cloudy or very dirty water also keeps light from reaching the plants.

Fertilizing: Aquarium plants must be fertilized if they are to remain healthy and grow. Aquarium stores sell excellent fertilizers for aquatic plants. Once a week, add the amount indicated on the package.

Fertilizers affect water quality negatively. For this reason, in freshly set-up tanks, where balanced conditions have yet to be established, you should not fertilize for the first three or four weeks.

Important: Never use fertilizers designed for indoor plants in an aquarium! They are deadly for aquarium fish.

Plant Care

Removing wilted leaves: These not only cause water quality to deteriorate but also withdraw nutrients from the plant. Cut wilted leaves off regularly with scissors, or nip them off with your fingernails. They can be pulled off only from unattached floating plants.

Thinning: Periodically you will need to thin plants that grow too vigorously. With stem plants that are set in the substrate, you can simply cut or nip off the unwanted shoots. *Echinodorus*, *Cryptocoryne*, and some other, similar plants may multiply so quickly, however, that some of them will have to be removed to keep the stand from becoming too thick.

The Proper Diet

The food requirements of live-bearers vary greatly among different species. On one end of the scale are the pure vegetarians; on the other, species that eat nothing but live fish. Luckily most live-bearers stay healthy in an aquarium if given generally available fish food. Indeed, many species accept dry food as the basic staple of their diet, and some can even be bred on it. To truly thrive, however, almost all species of live-bearers should get live food at least once or twice a week.

Dry Food

For the aquarist the easiest way of feeding fish is to give them dry food. It comes in various shapes, namely, flakes, tablets, pellets, and granules.

Dry food contains all the vitamins and trace elements fish need to stay healthy. Unfortunately, however, vitamins and trace elements deteriorate over time. For this reason you should observe the following rules:
- Buy dry food only in amounts that will be used up within about two months.
- If possible, buy brand-name products. These generally have a quicker turnover in stores, and their manufacturers are careful about the composition of ingredients.
- Look carefully at the box. Food can get stale in the store, and dusty packages are a telltale sign.

Food flakes: Food flakes come in an almost bewildering variety. They vary in the composition of ingredients, the size of the flakes, and the size of the package.

The most generally available kinds of food flakes consist of a combination of animal and vegetable substances. Thus they offer something for practically every fish species, no matter what its food preferences in the wild. Most live-bearers will stay healthy for quite a long time if fed this kind of food flakes, although you should supplement their diet with live food (see page 31). There are also food flakes that consist mostly of vegetable matter.

These are suitable primarily for live-bearers that live on vegetation in the wild (see "Some Popular Live-bearers and Instructions for Their Care," page 56). Some flakes contain color substances such as carotene, which enhances especially the red tints of the fish. These flakes are therefore a good addition to the normal diet of red varieties of fish.

The size of the flakes should always be in keeping with the size of your fish. If you have a community tank, you can use normal fish food flakes, which are a mixture of small and larger flakes and thus contain something for every size fish. But the smaller the fish in your tank, the smaller the flakes must be. Manufacturers produce food flakes suitable for every fish size.

If you are keeping baby fish together with adult fish in the same tank, crumble some of the flakes between your fingertips; in that way there will be enough tiny bits for the baby fish.

My Tip: If you want to intensify the red color of swordtails or platys, feed them paprika powder once a week. Paprika is particularly rich in carotene.

Food tablets: Food tablets come in two versions: those that immediately sink to the bottom, and those that are to be pressed against the aquarium glass, where they gradually dissolve. The first kind is suitable only for fish that feed on the bottom, and not all live-bearers do (see instructions for care, page 56). Most fish like food tablets that are stuck on the tank wall. Food tablets are a good addition to the diet of many live-bearers.

Food pellets: Food pellets consist of chopped up "threads" of dry food—something like miniature spaghetti—that are pressed together in pellet form. When crushed, the pellets form an excellent rearing food. However, food pellets should be used sparingly because they pollute the water. Special food pellets for ornamental fish are now also on the market, but in my experience these are not suitable as a rearing food and even larger fish are not fond of them.

The Proper Diet

Food granules: Food granules are excellent, but not all fish will eat them right away. Here, too, you have to be careful not to give too much (see "Eight Feeding Rules," page 36) because the granules, unlike flakes, don't decompose quickly but become moldy instead.

My Tip: If juvenile or adult fish refuse to eat a kind of food that is good for them, a day or two of fasting will help make the food appear more palatable.

Live Food

Live food is part of the natural diet of most live-bearers. Even so-called vegetarians and algae eaters absorb animal organisms that live in the algae. For this reason you should offer all live-bearers some live food at least once a week and preferably more often. Some species live primarily on live food (see instructions for care, page 56). Live food comes in four forms:
- fresh live food (live food animals)
- frozen live food
- dried live food
- freeze-dried live food

Fresh Live Food

In nature, fish often have to work hard for their food. They need to do a lot of chasing after potential prey before catching a meal. The pursuit provides good exercise and prevents the fish from getting fat, a condition common in aquarium fish (especially fat deposits in the liver). For aquarium fish, which ordinarily suffer from lack of exercise, chasing after live food animals presents an opportunity to swim hard. Live food animals are also healthful for the fish because they contain a lot of vitamins and trace elements, as well as roughage and important nutrients.

For these reasons you should make an effort to obtain live food animals for your fish at least occasionally.

Where You Can Get Live Animals

There are three ways of procuring live animals: you can collect them yourself, buy them, or raise them.

Collecting food animals: Food animals that live in water should come from bodies of water that contain no fish and that are as clean as possible;

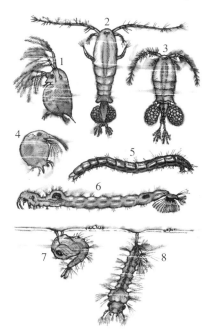

Food animals. Live food animals are an essential part of a healthy diet for live-bearers. You can either collect the food animals depicted here yourself or buy them at pet stores. (1) Water flea (*Daphnia*); (2) *Diaptomus* female with egg sacs; (3) *Cyclops* female with egg sacs; (4) *Bosmina*; (5) red mosquito larva (*Chironomos*); (6) white mosquito larva (*Corethra*); (7) pupa and (8) larva of the biting mosquito (*Culex*; black mosquito larva).

31

The Proper Diet

otherwise you may be introducing pathogens or parasites (fish lice, leeches) into your tank. Even in waters without fish you have to be careful not to inadvertently pick up freshwater polyps (genus *Hydra*) or eddy worms (planarians). These two primitive aquatic animals like to attack fry, and even some full-grown fish can suffer real damage from the stinging cells on the tentacles of freshwater polyps. Only a few live-bearers, particularly some Mexican topminnows, eat *Hydra*.

You should make it a rule to sift through the live food immediately right where you catch it. Larger creatures, such as dragonfly and predaceous diving beetle larvae (both are predatory and represent a danger to the inhabitants of an aquarium) and back swimmers, should be picked out and thrown back.

There are only a few live food animals that don't live in water and that you can collect yourself. Among them are flies. You don't have to worry about the legality of collecting them (see "Caution," below), and there is no danger of their transmitting diseases to the fish.

My Tip: Place food animals you have caught in a 5-gallon (20-L) tank with vigorously aerated water for half an hour. Reserve the tank for this sole purpose. After half an hour the freshwater polyps, planarians, and leeches will have attached themselves to the tank walls, and the suitable food animals are now clean and can be picked out.

Caution: Before you go out hunting for food animals, you should inquire about possible environmental regulations and should find out who owns the land that abuts on waters where you plan to gather food animals. Local aquarium clubs are a good source of information on where to collect live food animals.

Buying food animals: The simplest way of obtaining live food animals is to purchase them at an aquarium store. Tubifex worms, water fleas, and white mosquito larvae are usually available year round.

Raising food animals: One method that assures you of a constant supply of live, high-quality food animals is to raise them yourself (see page 34). Not many aquarists are taking advantage of this method. Of course, it does require extra time, but the great advantage is that you are no longer dependent on what can be found in nature and what is available at dealers.

Suitable Food Animals

Depending on the requirements of the particular species (see instruction for care, page 56), quite a large assortment of food animals may be suitable for feeding live-bearers. Only the most important ones can be mentioned in this small book. The literature listed on page 70 provides further information on this subject.

Mosquito larvae: There are three kinds of mosquito larvae, which are distinguished from each other by their colors, namely black, white, and red.

Black mosquito larvae can be found from spring to fall in small bodies of water and even in tiny puddles, often in the woods. The larvae are just below the water surface. Depending on their stage of development, they may be excellent food for fry as well as for adult live-bearers. But don't give the fish more larvae than they will consume within a few minutes, for black mosquito larvae grow into stinging mosquitoes (*Culex*) and may pupate within a few hours if the temperature is high enough (as in an aquarium). The fish are not fond of eating pupae (recognizable by their broad heads); and, I'm sure, you wouldn't want to have mosquitoes hatching in your living room.

My Tip: If you want to make absolutely sure the larvae won't hatch, put them in the freezer briefly (see Frozen Live Food, page 34) before feeding them to the fish. The fish will still eat them happily. You can also raise black mosquito larvae yourself. Put a big container of water—a planter or fish tank holding at least 12 gallons (50 L)—in a shady spot in your garden or on your balcony, and add some nettle juice (from crushed nettles). You

The Proper Diet

won't have to wait long before mosquito larvae will show up. Always skim the larvae off before they pupate.

White mosquito larvae are transparent rather than white. They are the larvae, not of true mosquitoes, but of a nonbitting phantom midge (*Corethra*), swarms of which are sometimes encountered on warm summer days. These larvae can be collected from clean, stagnant water. Especially in winter one often finds lots of them, even beneath a sheet of ice. White mosquito larvae make a very good fish food. They can be stored in the refrigerator wrapped in damp newspaper. Never feed these larvae to fry, however, because the larvae are predatory and may kill tiny fry.

Red mosquito larvae, too, are really the larvae of a nonbitting midge (*Chironomos*). You have to be cautious in using them because they occur mostly in the bottom mud of waters polluted with large amounts of organic matter or even with heavy metals. For this reason you should not give them to your fish more than once a week. Some live-bearers, such as guppies and Mexican topminnows, are especially fond of red mosquito larvae.

Caution: Contact with red mosquito larvae can give rise to strong allergic reactions in some people. Therefore, anyone subject to allergies should wear rubber gloves when handling the larvae and be careful to prevent contact with eyes and mucous membranes.

Small crustaceans: The most common small crustaceans are daphnia, a kind of water flea. They occur in many bodies of stagnant, clean to moderately dirty water. Daphnia are an excellent fish food, not very nutritious but containing lots of roughage, which keeps fish healthy. Certain daphnia are sometimes also found in garden pools. There are other suitable water fleas, such as the *Cyclops* and the *Bosmina* genera. Unfortunately *Cyclops* species, too, are predatory and, because they grow so fast, can endanger fry. *Bosmina* fleas are an almost ideal rearing food for fish, but they are found only rarely in natural bodies of water.

Worms: Tubifex worms are eagerly consumed by all live-bearers, and they are an excellent high-nutrition food, especially for breeding fish. They can also be chopped up and given to fry. Unfortunately, tubifex occur only in waters with high concentrations of organic matter (and often with other substances, including heavy metals). There these red worms live in the bottom mud, often forming dense colonies. You can also buy them at most pet stores. Whether you buy them or collect them yourself, tubifex have to be watered for several days before being given to your fish. Place the container with the worms under a slowly dripping faucet, or change the water several times a day, refilling the container again every time until the clump of worms is almost completely submerged. White tubifex, which are dead, and dirt must be removed before the worms are fed to the fish. Well-run pet stores sell only tubifex that have already been watered.

Feeding rings developed especially for tubifex are available from dealers. Be sure to use these if your aquarium does not include bottom-dwelling fish or large snails that will eat the worms that sink to the bottom.

My Tip: You can keep a small quantity of tubifex fresh for several days if you place them in the refrigerator, covered with water in a shallow dish. Change the water twice daily.

Note: Instructions for raising microworms are given on page 34.

Flies: Some live-bearers that live close to the water surface (see instructions for care, page 56) have specialized in catching flying insects, such as flies. It is possible to improve the health and longevity of these fish by including flies in their diet.

Small fruit flies are easiest to catch. Put a piece of fruit (banana works especially well) in an open canning jar in the summer and put the jar outside. After a few hours enough fruit flies will have congregated in the jar. Screw the cover on. If you would like to raise fruit flies, instructions follow.

The Proper Diet

Some Food Animals You Can Raise

You can raise some food animals of high nutritive value with a minimum investment in time. Starter cultures can be obtained from pet stores, through aquarium clubs, or from sources advertised in specialized magazines (see Useful Literature and Addresses, page 70).

Artemia Nauplii

The larvae of brine shrimp (*Artemia salina*) not only are a prime rearing food for baby fish but also are appreciated by many larger live-bearers. *Artemia* eggs stay viable for several years and are thus always available for the production of live food.

Rearing container: A 1- to 2-quart (1- to 2-L) bottle with a narrow neck. Close the bottle with a special *Artemia*-culture top (available from pet dealers) that has two openings: one through which air is blown into the bottle, and another through which air escapes.

Starter culture: 1 quart (1 L) water, 2 teaspoons salt without iodine, up to 3 teaspoons *Artemia* eggs (no more than the fish will consume within 2 days). Place the bottle in a warm place, about 77°F (25°C).

Aerate the mixture well with a membrane pump. Remove the nauplii (crustacean larvae) after about 24 hours.

Removal: Stop the membrane pump for a few minutes. Suck the clearly visible *Artemia* nauplii up with a small hose, and place them into a special *Artemia* sieve (available from aquarium dealers). Whatever salt is still contained in the nauplii will not harm the fish. Within three days the last nauplii should be consumed because by then the larvae will have nearly depleted their yolk sacs and will be nutritionally almost worthless.

Microworms

Mircoworms are easy to raise and make an excellent food for fry.

Rearing container: A small plastic or glass dish with a well-fitting top. Place a slice of bread in the dish, and add the microworm culture. Close the container, and let it stand for a few days. By that time the small worms, 0.08 inch (2 mm), will show up on the walls of the dish.

Removal: Remove the worms from the sides of the dish with your fingers or a small brush, and give them to the fish. Reserve some worms for breeding more.

Fruit Flies

Both the normal fruit fly (*Drosophila melanogaster*) and the Afghan fruit fly can be raised. Both species have strains with stunted wings that make flight impossible.

Rearing container: A glass jar holding at least 13 ounces (400 ml).

Food mush: Cook oat flakes, banana, and baby formula in a 1:1:1 proportion together with water to form a thick mush. Spread about ½ inch (1 cm) of the mush in the bottom of the jar, and top with crumpled paper for the hatched flies to crawl up on. Twenty flies are enough to start with. Cover the jar tightly with a material through which air presses freely, such as a piece of nylon stocking. After two weeks the flies are ready to use.

Removal: Shake the flies from the jar above the tank water. First remove enough flies to start another batch.

My Tip: Always keep two cultures going. If one should get moldy or if something else should go wrong, you will still have the other one.

Frozen Live Food

Frozen food is nutritionally almost as valuable as fresh food. You can buy bars of frozen live food

The Proper Diet

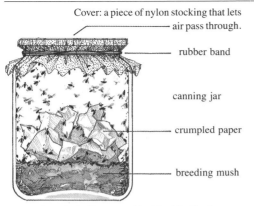

Cover: a piece of nylon stocking that lets
air pass through.

rubber band

canning jar

crumpled paper

breeding mush

Raising flies. Fruit flies are an ideal food for live bearers.

at pet or aquarium stores, or freeze the food yourself. If you do the freezing, treat the food in the same way you treat frozen food for yourself. The freezer must be at the proper temperature before you put in the food animals so that they freeze instantly. If kept at the right temperature, –5°F (–20°C), frozen food keeps its full nutritive value for one to two years.

Food animals such as black, red, and white mosquito larvae, water fleas, *Artemia* (adult), krill, and opossum shrimp can all be frozen. Black and white mosquito larvae, in particular, are an excellent supplement to the diet of larger live-bearers. You can also give any of the other food animals listed above once or twice a week. Tubifex worms should not be frozen.

Mussels and red meat (beef heart) freeze well but are eaten by only a few live-bearers, and therefore it is not worth bothering with these foods.

Dried Live Food

Occasionally, dried water fleas can still be seen in stores. These were an emergency food for aquarium fish in our grandfather's time. Using them now is not recommended, for dried food animals are almost worthless nutritionally.

Freeze-dried Live Food

Stores also sell freeze-dried mosquito larvae and tubifex worms. Most of my fish eat these mosquito larvae quite happily, but be careful: even in this form, red mosquito larvae can cause allergic reactions (see page 33). Freeze-dried tubifex are less popular than larvae and therefore don't contribute much toward a healthy diet.

Vegetable Foods

Some live-bearers live on a diet especially high in plant matter (see instructions for care, page 56). Algae are a nutritious vegetarian food. Place a canning jar filled with tank water in a sunny window, and add a few leaves from aquatic plants. The leaves will quickly become covered with algae. Many live-bearers, especially Mexican topminnows, also like scalded spinach leaves, chopped fine.

Feeding Fry

Foods suitable for fry are *Artemia* nauplii, *Bosmina* fleas, freshly hatched black mosquito larvae, chopped tubifex worms, microworms, and finely crushed dry food. Give fry only food that is no larger than the diameter of their eyes.

Feeding Fish You Want to Breed

To reduce the interval between broods and to increase the number of young, live food is given to breeding fish several times a week. Breeding fish need a very varied diet. Black mosquito larvae seem to have an especially positive effect on the number of young per brood.

The Proper Diet

Eight Feeding Rules

1. Feed only as much as the fish will consume within 15 minutes, unless you have bottom-dwelling fish or *Ampullaria* snails in the tank that will clean up the leftovers. Feed moderately even if there are scavengers in the tank.

2. Feed adult fish one or twice a day; growing fish, more often.

3. Institute a weekly fasting day for adult and older juvenile fish.

4. Never feed fish shortly before turning off the lights. Food that is not eaten in the evening will spoil during the night.

5. Add a variety to your fish's diet. Fish, like people, don't enjoy eating the same food all the time.

6. Make up a menu plan for a one- or two-week period.

7. Give your fish some live food at least once a week. Breeding fish should get live food several times a week.

8. Siphon up food that remains in the aquarium an hour after feeding; otherwise, the water quality will deteriorate to an unacceptable level.

Diseases of Live-bearers

Live-bearers are susceptible to only a few diseases; on the whole they don't get sick much. Diseases are caused by bacteria, viruses, and parasites in the tank, but healthy fish generally have enough immunity to fight off pathogens. Unfavorable conditions, such as wrong or inadequate diet, poor water quality, overcrowding, and other situations causing stress, can, however, weaken live-bearers enough so that they may get sick. In this chapter the most common diseases of live-bearers are described. Of course, a number of other diseases may also occur. For further information, please consult the appropriate literature (see page 70).

Avoiding Disease

You can prevent many diseases from breaking out among your live-bearers by offering the fish optimal living conditions. There are also a few important rules that you should observe.
- Don't buy or introduce into your tank any fish that are visibly sick (see "Is Quarantine Absolutely Necessary?" on page 12).
- Place sick fish in a separate tank for treatment.
- Remove dead fish immediately.
- Check your fish daily for signs of illness.
- Treat sick fish promptly. The sooner treatment is initiated, the better the chances for recovery.

My Tip: Always keep medications for the most common diseases on hand, so that you can start treating your fish immediately, even on a weekend.
- Disinfect catching nets and other utensils after every use if you have more than one tank. You can use a salt solution made of 1 quart (1 L) water and 3 1/2 ounces (100 g) salt, or you can buy a methylene blue solution from a pharmacist.

Important: Nets and other accessories that have been disinfected must be rinsed clean under clear water.

Diseases That Are Fairly Common

For the diseases described in this section there are effective drugs that can be obtained from pet dealers or from pharmacists. Always be sure to follow the directions that come with the drugs.

Caution: Always store fish medications in a place that is inaccessible to children.

White Spot Disease or "Ich"

Signs of illness: Small, white dots up to 1/24 inch (1 mm) in diameter on skin and fins.

Cause: Ciliate protozoan (*Ichthyophthirius*).

Treatment: Commercially available drugs, used as prescribed in the directions that come with the product.

Cotton-wool Disease or Mouth Fungus

Signs of illness: A white film on the mouth and along the outer edges of the fins. In guppies, especially, the fins become frayed.

Cause: A bacterial infection (*Flexibacter columnaris*).

Treatment: Partial water change; then treat with Maracyn or a similar drug, following instructions for use. Mild cases can be treated with salt (NaCl, noniodized) or potassium permanganate. Infected fish should be isolated. Kill badly infected fish that have lost entire fins (see page 40).

Bacterial Fin Rot

Signs of illness: Frayed fins that have a broad, whitish band along the edges; occasionally the entire fin is stuck together.

Cause: Bacterial infection (*Pseudomonas*, *Aeromonas*, and other bacteria).

Treatment: Immediate improvement of environmental conditions, together with a broad-spectrum antibiotic as prescribed in the instructions for use. Treatment of choice is with nitro-

Diseases of Live-bearers

furazone or a combination of nitrofurazone and furazolidone.

Fish Tuberculosis

Signs of illness: Protuberant scales, bulging eyes, external tumors, dramatic weight loss, ascites (bloating of the body).

Cause: Bacterial infection (*Mycobacterium* spp.).

Treatment: Once the disease has reached the visible stage, no treatment is likely to be successful. Kill infected fish (see page 40). Fish tuberculosis practically never occurs in fish that are kept under optimal conditions!

Caution: Fish tuberculosis can cause minor infections in humans (pimples that don't want to heal on parts of the body that come into contact with the aquarium water). Therefore, you should never reach into the water if the skin is broken on your hands unless you are wearing rubber gloves.

Gill Flukes

Signs of illness: Fish hang just below the water surface with gill covers open, breathing heavily, or rub their gills against rocks or decorative objects.

Cause: Gill flukes (*Dactylogyrus* or *Gyrodactylus*).

Treatment: A praziquantel bath is the treatment of choice for gill flukes (dactylogyridae). Since praziquantel eliminates both gill and body flukes safely, it should probably be used more often in place of dylox. If, however, praziquantel is not available, gill flukes on wild-caught fishes can be eradicated with a dylox bath. Ask your pet shop manager for more details.

Intestinal Worms

Signs of illness: Emaciation; stringy, whitish excreta. Occasionally red worms can be seen hanging from the anus.

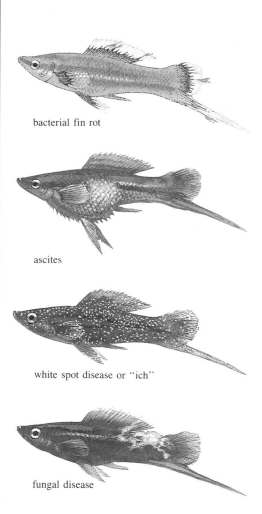

bacterial fin rot

ascites

white spot disease or "ich"

fungal disease

Fish Diseases
The diseases of live-bearers depicted here are caused by bacteria, viruses, and parasites. Fish most likely to succumb to disease are those that are already weakened because of stress and unfavorable living conditions, such as incorrect diet, poor water quality, and overcrowding in the tank.

38

Diseases of Live-bearers

Cause: Threadworms (*Capillaria*) or parasitical nematodes (*Camallanus*).

Treatment: Difficult. Concurat or Masoten may be effective. Mix Concurat into the food or feed it directly, but no more than twice in a row; then wait 3 weeks before repeating the treatment.

Cloudy Skin

Signs of illness: Milky film on skin and fins; gummed up fins; fish hang in water rocking back and forth.

Cause: Flagellates (*Costia*) or ciliates (*Chilodonella*).

Treatment: Raise water temperature to 90°F (32°C), or use drugs containing methylene blue, available from pet dealers.

Poisoning

Signs of illness: Fish hang just below water surface gasping for air, even though filtration and aeration are functioning properly. Sometimes the fish dash around the aquarium erratically.

What Is Wrong With These Live-bearers?

Changes in Behavior or Appearance	Possible Cause	Treatment
Gasping for air at the water surface	1. Oxygen deficiency due to malfunctioning of filter or aeration	Immediately change half the water; repair filter/aerator.
	2. Gill flukes	See page 38.
	3. Water too warm	Check temperature.
Rubbing against objects in the tank	1. Gill flukes	See page 38.
	2. White spot disease	See page 37.
	3. Cloudy skin	See above; improve conditions.
Rocking in the water	1. Cloudy skin	See above.
	2. Bacterial fin rot	See page 37; improve conditions.
Emaciation	1. Intestinal disease	Use medication.
	2. Fish tuberculosis	Kill fish.
Frantic dashing around in the water	1. Poisoning	Change half the water; check water properties.
	2. Dermal parasites	Watch fish carefully; use drugs if indicated.
Inability to swim properly, or lying on the bottom	Damaged swim bladder caused by being too cold	Check fish carefully; supply varied diet; check water properties.
Frayed fins	1. White spot disease	See page 37.
	2. Bacterial fin rot	See page 37.
	3. Other fish that are aggressive	Observe the fish population.

Diseases of Live-bearers

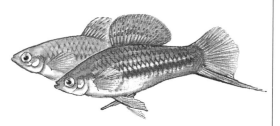

Courtship display of Cortez swordtails. The male "dances" around the female with widely spread fins.

Cause: Metal poisoning through copper (new pipes, too much algae killer) or through organic waste products, such as ammonia or nitrite (see page 23).

Treatment: Make sure the population density is very low in a newly set up tank; change the water regularly. In an acute case of poisoning, take these immediate measures: change half of the water; repeat after 12 hours if necessary. Determine the cause (aquarium stores sell test sets).

Some Important Points about Treating Diseases

Importance of prompt treatment: You should always try to identify and treat a disease at the first sign of illness you observe. Most fish diseases can be cured at this early stage. If possible, use drugs obtained from specialized pet dealers. Some people recommend using antibiotics for fish; but I am opposed to this practice. Mass breeders of tropical fish in export countries overuse antibiotics, and some pathogens have already developed an immunity to them. In addition, fish diseases that require treatment with antibiotics are generally incurable.

A note about activated charcoal: While using medications, you should stop filtering with activated charcoal. After successful treatment has been concluded, however, you will need to filter again with activated charcoal to remove the medication still left in the water.

Killing a Fish

If a fish has to be killed because it is sick, do it quickly. The best method, especially for small species, is to submerge the fish in boiling water. If you can't bring yourself to do this, sever the spine quickly, using a razor blade, immediately behind the head. In this way the fish will not suffer unnecessarily.

Breeding Live-bearers

Breeding live-bearers not only is a fascinating hobby but also teaches you a lot about fish. The young fry are able to swim immediately after birth (see drawing, page 6). They require no parental care. In fact, for some species, such as the Mexican topminnows, it is important that the fry have somewhere to hide within their first seconds of life because the parents try to eat them as soon as they are born.

Breeding to Multiply Fish or Selective Breeding?

In the case of live-bearers there are two distinct purposes of breeding.

Breeding to increase the number of fish is what must hobbyists aspire to. To accomplish this aim, you have to provide living conditions favorable enough for the fish to reproduce and give birth to healthy offspring.

Selective breeding also has as its goal the production of healthy fish. But in addition the breeder attempts to influence the color, the shape of the fins, and the body shape of the fish by carefully selecting the parent animals (see page 48). Through this kind of controlled breeding, new forms are developed that do not occur in nature. You will find more on this topic in the chapter "Well-known Ornamental Varieties," which starts on page 47.

Selecting the Breeding Stock

Regardless of your purpose in breeding, you should observe two basic rules in selecting the fish to be bred.

Select only healthy fish! A fish with visible defects, such as a curved spine or malformed fins, is not suitable for breeding. You should also not use excessively slender fish (see "Fish Tuberculosis," page 38) for breeding.

Breeding method: If you would like to raise a lot of young fish all at once, you can let several females spawn one after another in this kind of net construction. The fry slip through the net into the rearing tank after they are born.

Select fish of the right age! For live-bearers the ideal age for breeding is—depending on the species—from one to two years old. You can use young fish as soon as they reach sexual maturity (at 3 to 9 months, depending on the species), but the number of young per brood is much smaller than with full-grown fish. Also, it is generally hard to tell whether live-bearers that are not fully mature will eventually reach the size and body shape you expect.

My Tip: Buy six to eight juvenile fish and raise them to maturity. Keep the best individuals for breeding, and give away or sell the rest.

Breeding in a Community or a Species Tank

Most live-bearers can be bred in either a community aquarium or a species tank. This is assuming, of course, that the species is not cannibalistic (see "Popular Live-bearers and Their Care," page 56) and that there are no other predatory species in the tank.

Breeding Live-Bearers

What can be a problem is providing the fry with sufficiently small food particles during the first few days. A tank that has been in operation for some time contains plenty of food for a small number of fry, but the amount is insufficient if you want to raise as many young fish as possible. Aiming food specifically at the fry is difficult because they scatter all over the tank quickly after birth. This means that you have to feed frequently to make sure that all the fry get enough to eat. Unfortunately, however, this can cause the water quality to deteriorate (see "Nitrite and Nitrate," page 23).

Spawning Boxes

A spawning box (available from stores) allows you to raise fry up to a certain size and to control their feeding. These boxes are hung in the maintenance tank.

Setup: Place some crystalwort (*Riccia*) on top of the water to give the newly born fry a sense of safety.

Procedure: Place the pregnant female in the box (see page 43). The young slip down through a grill into the lower part of the box and thus are safe from being eaten by a cannibalistic mother. After the female has given birth, she can be returned to the maintenance tank and the grill in the spawning box is removed.

Disadvantage: Unfortunately the spawning boxes available at aquarium stores are much too small. The base generally measures only about 8 × 4 inches (20 × 10 cm). Larger live-bearers— swordtails, for instance—often injure fins and mouths on the boxes because they keep bumping into the walls. Occasionally, too, a female will enter a state of permanent stress and give birth prematurely before the young are viable. Smaller species of live-bearers give birth in these boxes without problems, but another difficulty can arise.

One brood often consists of 30 to 50 young. Such a number of fry soon becomes too crowded in the small box, and the young fry fail to grow and thrive properly.

My Tip: If you are at all handy with tools, you can easily copy a commercial model and build a spawning box yourself. The base should be at least 12 × 8 inches (30 × 20 cm), and the height should be about 6 inches (15 cm). The maintenance aquarium in which the box is hung has to be about three times this size.

A Breeding Tank

I personally recommend getting a separate breeding tank for the young to be born and raised in.

Size: For small species up to 1½ inches (4 cm), a tank holding between 2½ and 5 gallons (10 and 20 L) is big enough. Larger species, such as swordtails, can give birth in a 5-gallon (20-L) tank, but for raising the young it is advisable to have a tank holding at least 20 gallons (80 L).

Setup: Place some bushy aquarium plants, such as *Najas indica* or swordfern (*Microsorium pteropus*), in the tank. The plants cut down some of the female's freedom of movement, and the newly born fry can find food and shelter among the plants.

Technical equipment: Same as for a maintenance tank (see page 22).

Water: Same as for a maintenance tank (see page 22). Females almost ready to give birth may react with extreme sensitivity to drastic changes in water properties, with the not-infrequent result that the young are born dead.

Procedure: Place the female in the breeding tank about a week before she is due to give birth (see page 43). After the young are born, return her to the maintenance tank.

Breeding Live-Bearers

An Efficient Breeding Method

If you want to let several species of live-bearers breed simultaneously or would like to raise a lot of fry (see "Rules to Prevent Unwanted Crossings," following), you can try the following breeding method, which involves a minimum of space and cost.

A tank of 25 gallons (100 L) or more is suitable. Attach a net to the top of the tank so that the net dips down into the water (see drawing, page 41), or fashion a tube out of plastic-covered wire mesh. Sew the mesh together with strong, nondyed thread. The tube should be about 4–8 inches (10–20 cm) in diameter and slightly longer than the water is deep. Place the tube on the bottom of the tank with the upper end sticking just barely out of the water. It is important that the gills and fins of the female cannot stick out through the spaces between the wires; therefore, the wires should be no more than 0.08 to 0.2 inch (2 to 5 mm) apart.

About a week before the females are due, place them in this tube or in the net, one at a time or—if the net or tube is large enough—several at once. Don't forget to cover the net or tube because many live-bearers are lively jumpers. The fry will be able to swim between the wires or through the weave of the net and thus will be safe from the predatory pursuit of the females. Return the females to the maintenance tank after they have given birth.

You won't need a new breeding tank until there are too many young or unless older juveniles are likely to eat newborn fry.

The Right Time to Isolate the Females

If you use a spawning box or breeding tank, a female should be taken from the maintenance tank about a week before she is due to give birth. But how can you tell when that time has come?

Gestation lasts about 4 weeks for fully mature females kept under optimal conditions. Females can be fertilized again immediately after giving birth, but the interval between broods can vary. The shortest period between broods is about 3 weeks. If conditions are not optimal, however, up to 5 months can elapse between broods. The instructions for care starting on page 56 include information on brood frequency.

Pregnancy is easiest to detect before feeding, for gravid females have noticeably rounder bellies than nongravid ones. In many species you can also tell by the so-called gravid spot (see page 11). Often you can see the silvery eyes of the young shimmering through this spot shortly before they will be born. When that is the case, it is time to move the mother to the breeding tank. In some species, such as mollies, however, it is difficult to tell just when the young are due. These fish have no gravid spot and don't increase much in girth. Here you have to rely on close observation. Wait until the female has given birth. Afterward she is bound to be thinner than before. If she then rounds out again, she has in all likelihood been reimpregnated and you can remove her to the breeding tank at the proper time.

A few species, such as the midget live-bearer (see page 59), do not follow this normal pattern. Instead of all the brood being born at once, only one to five young are born per day. The appearance of the young is spread out over a period of time that may last several weeks. This phenomenon is called superfetation.

My Tip: If a female does not give birth even though her girth indicates that she is due, it often helps to raise the water temperature by about 4°F (2°C).

Rules to Prevent Unwanted Crossings

If you engage in selective breeding (see page 47), you sometimes want to cross two different

Breeding Live-Bearers

species in order to achieve a certain breeding goal. This is not the case with wild strains; here crossings are never desirable. Members of different species do, however, crossbreed sometimes, even if potential partners of the proper species are present in the tank. To prevent such unwanted crossings, observe the following rules:

- Keep only species belonging to different genera in any one tank.
- Combine juvenile fish belonging to different species of the same genus only if you can tell the sexes apart reliably before the fish reach sexual maturity. It is safer not to combine such juveniles at all.
- If, in spite of your precautions, a batch of hybrids turns up, don't raise them.

Inbreeding

In some fish, inbreeding can be a real problem that interferes with successful reproduction, but this is generally not the case with live-bearers. In fact, for purposes of selective breeding it is sometimes necessary to resort to inbreeding of a strain for several generations in order to achieve the desired breeding goals.

Nevertheless, you should watch the fish you raise carefully for signs of inbreeding, especially if they have mated only with closely related fish for more than three generations. Possible signs of inbreeding are as follows:

- Physical malformations, such as curved spines and misshapen heads, are present.
- More than 10 percent of the young are dead at birth.
- Offspring are lacking even though the fish are kept under optimal conditions.
- The number of young is consistently smaller than normal (see instructions for care, page 56).
- The young fish fail to attain their parents' size in spite of optimal conditions and feeding.
- Almost all the fish die very young, often shortly before reaching sexual maturity.

Especially if several of these conditions are observed at once, you may be dealing with deterioration due to inbreeding. At this point you have only two alternatives: either you give up breeding this particular stock, or you cross your fish with different ones of the same species or (in the case of selective breeding) with others closely similar in appearance to the type of fish you wish to breed.

Raising the Fry

In general, the fry of live-bearers are easy to raise. Nevertheless, to make sure they will turn into healthy fish with which you can breed future generations, you have to observe three basic rules.

- Provide the optimal living conditions that fry and juvenile fish require. The young are more vulnerable than adult fish. Damage sustained through inadequate diet, for instance, cannot be remedied later on.

My Tip: When rearing fry, change a quarter of the tank water every week or, if necessary, more often.

- Feed the fry frequently. The absolute minimum is one feeding per day. If you have the time, feed these fish up to six times a day.

Important: Here, too, remember to give the fish no more food than they will consume within 15 minutes. Fry and juveniles react negatively to murky water, which is often the result of overfeeding.

- Provide the proper kind of food! Most fry need live food at least once a week (see instructions for care, page 56).

Four-eyed fish. The four-eyed fish (*Anableps anableps*) can see above and below water simultaneously because its eyes are subdivided. The teeth on the upper and lower lips are clearly visible.

Well-known Ornamental Varieties

What Is Selective Breeding?

Every fish hobbyist knows the famous lyre-tail guppy. Fish with such extravagant tails don't occur in nature; they are the result of years of breeding efforts on the part of humans. This kind of breeding is known as controlled or selective breeding. The resulting fish are ornamental forms.

Three criteria are of preeminent importance in the selective breeding of ornamental fish: fin shape, color, and body shape. The goal that one is attempting to achieve is defined before breeding is begun.

Which Live-bearers Are Suitable for Selective Breeding?

Not all fish species are suitable subjects for selective breeding. The most promising candidates are species in which deviations from the normal form occur with some frequency in nature. In other words, not all offspring of a species look exactly alike; they already exhibit variations in fin shape, color, or body shape. Other types of fish require hundreds of generations before mutation, such as a difference in color, becomes established under natural conditions. In live-bearers this can happen within a few generations.

Seven species of live-bearers belonging to two genera are the ones most suitable for selective breeding. They are the guppy (*Poecilia reticulata*), the molly (*P. sphenops*, *P. latipinna*, and *P. velifera*), the swordtail (*Xiphophorus helleri*), and the platy (*X. maculatus* and *X. variatus*).

Live-bearing toothed carps and Mexican topminnows. Above. Merry widows (*Phallichtys amates*). Below, left: *Xenotoca eiseni* belongs to the family of the Mexican topminnows (Goodeidae). Below, right: Male *Ameca splendens*, also a member of the Goodeidae family.

The Basics of Genetics

Anyone attempting selective breeding needs to acquire some background in genetics. To discuss this subject in any detail here would take up too much space. Please consult some of the literature on this subject listed in the bibliography (see page 70) or turn to an appropriate aquarists' society for help (for addresses, see page 70).

The physical appearance of fish is determined by their genes. When engaging in selective breeding, the breeder attempts to find out where on the chromosomes the genes of interest are located.

Dominant traits are easiest to manipulate. Dominance means that the desired trait shows up in the very first generation of offspring. Examples of such traits are the brushlike fin shape of platys (see page 53) and the lyre-shaped fins of swordtails (see drawing, page 16). If, for example, a wild-form platy is crossed with a brush-finned platy, 50 percent of the offspring will have brushlike fins.

Recessive or hidden traits are more complicated to deal with. Here the situation is easiest if one can find parents both of which have the recessive gene in question. Then 25 percent of the offspring will exhibit the desired trait. It is of course easier to continue breeding with these offspring. If a dominant gene that conceals the recessive one is introduced, however, the appearance of the offspring may be altered and the desired trait disappear in the next generation.

Not all the workings of genetic law are as simple to explain as these basic examples. To gain the necessary understanding, intensive study of genetics is usually required.

You can also get a sense of how genetics works by trial and error. Often, though, there are too many possible combinations. Moreover, you would have to keep all the offspring up to the second or third generation in order to see whether they have the desired genes, and this would not only be very time-consuming but also require a great deal of aquarium space.

Well-known Ornamental Varieties

Choosing Fish for Selective Breeding

When choosing your breeding stock, you need to pay attention not only to the criteria mentioned on page 41 but to other aspects as well. The situation is easiest if you have one or several pairs of fish that already have all the traits you are looking for. Then all you have to do is to weed out all inferior animals (see "Special Aspects of Selective Breeding," below).

Suitable breeding stock (a minimum of one pair) can often be purchased from a dealer or may be acquired from the American Live-bearer Association (see Addresses, page 70). Particularly in the case of guppies, however, obtaining breeding stock is not always easy. Some breeders sell only males, and you have to try to find females of a similar strain. Unfortunately you cannot tell by inspection whether female guppies belong to the desired strain. A larger, more colorful tail does indicate that a particular female belongs to the long-finned, rather than the ordinary short-finned, type, but often that is about the only clue external appearance gives.

Special Aspects of Selective Breeding

When attempting selective breeding, it is not enough to simply combine the parent fish in a tank, raise their offspring, and hope for positive results. Optimal living conditions, strict selection—that is, culling inferior specimens—and a knowledge of genetics are absolutely essential.

Culling is one of the crucial aspects that distinguishes selective breeding from breeding to merely increase the number of fish. To achieve a given breeding goal you must observe the strictest standards in mating successive generations, and you have to weed out, or cull, all fish that don't conform to the desired goal. Here, specifically, is what you need to do:

- Keep all young until they are at least half-grown and give a clear indication of their future physical appearance.
- Keep in mind that, even if a juvenile fish shows signs of having the desired traits, it cannot be used for breeding if it shows defects in other respects, such as abnormally small size or some other physical shortcoming.
- Pay special attention to the liveliness of the breeding fish and their offspring. Unfortunately, all too often, fish are bred that are hardly able to move because of their extravagantly large and heavy fins. Never forget that you are dealing with living creatures. Excesses should be avoided even in selective breeding.

My Tip: It is best to kill fish with physical defects (see page 40) or feed them to other fish. Many breeders of live-bearers keep some species, such as pike live-bearers (see page 57), that live entirely on live fish. Or you may be able to sell healthy offspring of your fish that don't conform to your breeding goal to a pet dealer and thus recover some of the cost of your hobby.

The Most Popular Ornamental Varieties

Selective breeding is such a large topic and there are so many ornamental strains that this subject could easily fill a separate volume. For this reason, I will introduce here only the most important and best-known ornamental varieties.

If you are interested in how these forms came about, you can read about them in publications of the various fish associations that deal specifically with selective breeding (see addresses, page 70).

Well-known Ornamental Varieties

The Guppy

The various ornamental forms of the guppy are among the best-known and most popular aquarium fish.

The guppy breeders of Europe have joined together and developed a common standard for breeding guppies. This standard defines the goals of selective breeding, such as the shape of the tail. The standard, by the way, sets the length of the fish, exclusive of tail, at 1 inch (26 mm).

Tail shapes: The standard accepts 12 different shapes, divided into two basic types: the short- and the long-tailed guppies. The short-tailed varieties can be bred directly from the wild form. In nature, too, there are guppies with short tails of various shapes. The round-tail guppy (see drawing, below), for instance, arose in this way.

In 1954 the American breeder Paul Hähnel created a sensation when he exhibited the first male lyre-tail guppy. Breeders in Southeast Asia, in particular, were quick to breed this mutation and did so very successfully. For many years they supplied world markets with excellent fish, but the guppies that come from Southeast Asia today no longer live up to those of earlier years. The reason may be that

Fin and Tail Shapes of Guppies

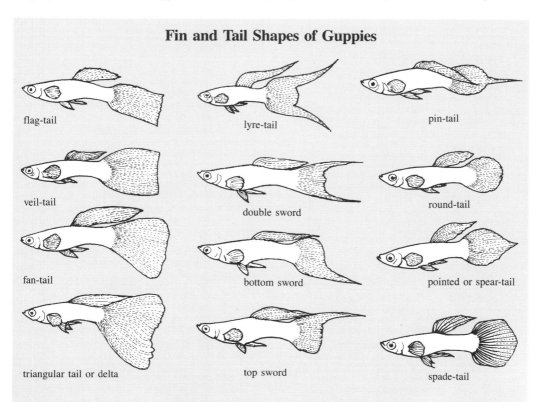

flag-tail

lyre-tail

pin-tail

veil-tail

double sword

round-tail

fan-tail

bottom sword

pointed or spear-tail

triangular tail or delta

top sword

spade-tail

they are kept in brackish water and given antibiotics and other drugs to prevent diseases. Apparently this regime weakens their resistance so much that many imported guppies don't survive long in normal aquariums.

My Tip: Pet stores often have male guppies with huge lyre-tails. In some fish the tail is so overdeveloped that it droops down and the fish can no longer swim properly. In my opinion such fish should not be used for breeding because these males are hardly able to perform proper courtship displays and to impregnate the female.

Ground and cover colors: In addition to fin shape, colors play an important role in selective breeding.

Guppies have a basic or ground color on which there are markings in other, bright and iridescent "cover" colors that catch the eye. The most important ground colors of guppies are wild-color, albino, blond, and blue.

- Wild-color guppies have the same gray or olive-green ground color as their cousins in nature. Most of the guppies bred and sold in Europe are of this color.
- Albinos lack black pigments in their bodies. The body is light-colored, and the eyes are red. In contrast to many other albinos, whose bodies are flesh-colored, male guppy albinos can have various cover colors, such as red, white, and cream.
- Blond guppies also have light-colored bodies. In them the black pigment is much reduced but not completely lacking. They have dark eyes. The males may have darker cover colors than albino males. Blond guppies are quite commonly sold and kept in Europe.
- Blue guppies lack shades of yellow and red and therefore have a bluish shimmer. They are very rare because they are hard to distinguish from wild-color strains.
- By combining these colors, other ground colors can be created.

There is hardly a color that may not turn up as a cover color. Inventive breeders keep producing new cover colors through different combinations.

The most popular cover color markings have been given names. Some examples are snakeskin, carpet pattern, and Vienna emerald (here the place where the variety originated is included in the name).

The Swordtail

As in the case of guppies, mutations occur with some frequency in swordtails living in the wild, and these mutations have provided the bases for many ornamental forms of swordtails.

Three different types are distinguished in the standard for swordtails: those with normal fins, those with tall fins, and those with lyre-shaped fins.

Normal fins: These fish have the same fin shapes as the wild form.

Tall fins: Only the shape of the dorsal fin has been modified through selective breeding. This fin is either flag-shaped or veil-like.

Lyre-shaped fins: In this type, the outer or first rays of all the fins are twice as long as the rest of the fin. The tail fin sports a double sword. This variety of swordtail is sometimes called the dragon swordtail. Unfortunately, the first fin rays of the gonopodium are almost always so elongated that the males are no longer able to impregnate females. The gene for lyre-shaped fins is dominant.

Ground and cover color: The ground colors of swordtails are essentially the same as those of guppies, except that there is no blue in swordtails. In these fish, the wild color is often described as green. Almost all of the various colors of swordtails have been achieved by cross-breeding between species and then breeding back to the original type.

Swordtails don't have as many different cover colors as guppies; apart from black markings, one

Well-known Ornamental Varieties

Ten Tips for the Selective Breeding of Guppies

1. The first step is to obtain several pairs of guppies that exhibit the desired traits (see page 49). Short-tailed females, unlike long-tailed ones, are without markings on the tail. The tails of long-tailed females are larger and colorful.

2. A beginner in the art of selective breeding should first build up a strain of uniform genetic makeup, that is, a strain in which all male offspring conform to the desired standard for several generations. Assume, for example, that the desired standard is a wild-color lyre-tail guppy with white as a cover color. If all the males display these traits over several generations and their offspring are healthy, you can assume that the strain is genetically uniform. The physical traits of the standard do not show up in the females, which is why you have to concentrate on the males.

3. To build up a genetically uniform strain, you need about seven tanks. If you take good care of the fish, tanks holding at least 6 gallons (25L) are big enough.

4. If you begin with a single pair, the female must be moved into a separate tank for the very first brood (see page 43).

5. The female should be returned to the maintenance tank as soon as she has given birth.

6. The best food on which to raise the fry is *Artemia* nauplii.

7. The young must be segregated by sex when they are four weeks old, before they reach sexual maturity. After all, you want to use for further breeding only the males that conform most closely to your ideal. It may take some practice before you can tell the sexes apart reliably. Watch for the first rays of the anal fin; these will later develop into the gonopodium and are already somewhat thicker than the rest at this point.

8. If you notice signs of inbreeding in your breeding stock (see page 44), you need to build up a second strain and occasionally swap individuals between the two strains. Experienced breeders generally start out with two strains for this reason. The parallel building up of identical breeding stocks is called line breeding. You need at least 14 tanks if you want to do line breeding.

9. It is better to take really good care of one strain than to attempt to keep ten strains going without achieving passable results. Don't spread yourself too thin!

10. A beginner should always seek the advice of an experienced breeder.

finds primarily red. In recent years, however, many swordtails with shades of orange have come on the market. They are called neon or pineapple swordtails.

Ornamental Swordtail Varieties

Some of the most popular swordtail varieties have been named after the German cities where they were first bred.

Berlin cross-breed (see drawing on page 24): This is a red swordtail with black spots. If members of this variety are mated with each other, however, the offspring often develop melanomata (a kind of tumor). These fish are not suitable for further breeding. To perpetuate the variety, a red swordtail with black spots is mated with a plain red one.

Frankfurt cross-breed (see drawing on page 53): The front half of the fish is red; the back half is black and sharply set off from the front.

Well-known Ornamental Varieties

Ten Tips for the Selective Breeding of Swordtails

1. You can often find attractive pairs of swordtails in pet stores, but make sure their colors match.

2. The females have the same fin shapes as the males and must display the same markings. The sword of the male, however, is almost always rimmed with black.

3. You should begin by building a genetically uniform breeding stock (see page 48). If you buy a swordtail pair, you never know the exact genetic makeup of the fish. Don't be surprised, therefore, if some of the offspring bear no resemblance to their parents. By rigorously culling nonconforming offspring, you can still achieve your breeding goal.

4. You will need large tanks holding at least 20 gallons (80 L) for breeding.

5. In a species tank with plenty of plants (see page 13) the female doesn't necessarily have to be isolated before giving birth. If you want to breed efficiently, though, it is better to let the female give birth in a breeding tank.

6. If several juvenile swordtails grow up together in a shoal, a rank hierarchy will emerge. The strongest male will develop a sword before the rest, whose sword development is inhibited. Don't be disappointed, there-fore, if out of ten males only one looks really splendid. If the strongest male is removed from the shoal, the next strongest will develop the biggest sword.

7. Since males fight fiercely among each other, you should keep only one, or else at least about five of approximately equal strength, in a tank.

8. If you keep giving away superfluous males and females and those that don't fit in with your breeding plans, you can do selective breeding with just one tank.

9. Some males are precocious in developing their gonopodiums and swords. These fish remain small and slender for the rest of their lives. Others look like females at first and acquire the male characteristics only when fully grown. These fish generally have small swords in relation to their body size but are much stronger than other males. I prefer these late bloomers for breeding; they are less susceptible to disease and often have more beautiful colors.

10. If you want to obtain lyre-finned swordtails, you need to mate a normal-finned male with a lyre-finned female. Fifty percent of the offspring will have lyre-shaped fins.

Hamburg cross-breed (see drawing, page 53): The fins are yellowish, and the body is as completely black as possible. On the sides of the body there are shiny scales with a greenish or bluish metallic sheen.

Wiesbaden cross-breed: The sides of the body, down into the tail, are black with shiny scales. The back and abdomen are green or red.

Green swordtail: The body is green with a red lateral, zigzag band.

Red swordtail: A dark red cover color overlays the ground color, which is also red. The fish are thus completely red (except for the sword of the male). In the rare red albino even the eyes and the male's sword are red.

Important varieties with black markings: The tuxedo and the wagtail are two well-known varieties with black markings. In tuxedos, the sides of the body (but not the tail fin) are about two-thirds completely black without shiny scales. In

Well-known Ornamental Varieties

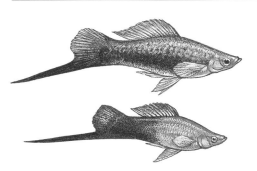

Ornamental swordtail varieties. The Frankfurt cross-breed (bottom) and the Hamburg cross-breed (above) look very attractive.

wagtails, all the fins (except the ventral and anal fins) are pure black. In addition, there are swordtail varieties with the same black markings that are found in maculatus platys (see drawing, page 53).

The Platy

Platy varieties fall into two groups corresponding to the two species that occur in the wild (see "Popular Live-bearers and Their Care," page 56). They are the maculatus and the variatus platys.

Maculatus Platys
The standard for maculatus platys calls for the fish to be especially deep-bodied. There should be no noticeable break between body and tail. Males grow to a length of 1½ inches (4 cm); females, to 2 ³/₈ inches (6 cm).

My Tip: Exceptionally large platys are likely to have been crossed with swordtails a few generations back, and the strain has not yet been bred back to purity. Caution is in order when buying such fish.

Fin shape: Almost all platys have tall dorsal fins, with the fin being either flaglike or quadrant-shaped. There is also a special strain with a brushlike tail. In these platys the central rays of the tail fin are elongated to form a point. The gene for this type of tail is dominant.

Ground and cover colors: The ground colors are the same as in swordtails (see page 50). The cover colors are red, blue, marigold, and black.

A few black markings and color variations in platys are especially well known (see drawing on page 54). These ornamental platys are as follows:

Comet platy: The upper and lower edges of the tail fin are black.

Two-spot platy: There is a small dot at the top and at the bottom where the tail fin begins.

Half-moon platy: The tail fin is set off from the body by a crescent-shaped band.

Moon platy: There is a large, round, black spot on the caudal peduncle.

Pepper-and-salt platy: The entire body and the fins are covered with black dots.

Blue mirror platy: The ground color is gray, with shiny blue scales on the sides of the body.

Coral platy: One vertebra is lacking, and the fish is therefore especially deep-bodied. Males and females are dark red.

Bleeding-heart platy: The blond male has a red breast, from which red bands emanate upward on the body. The females have a mere suggestion of red bands.

Note: Tuxedo and wagtail markings (see page 52) are also very common.

Variatus Platys
Variatus platys are among the most difficult species to breed selectively because they grow very slowly and you can't tell until late in their development whether they correspond to the type you are trying to breed. For this reason dealers charge more for them than for maculatus platys. The standard calls for the same physical characteristics that apply to maculatus platys. Both male and

Well-known Ornamental Varieties

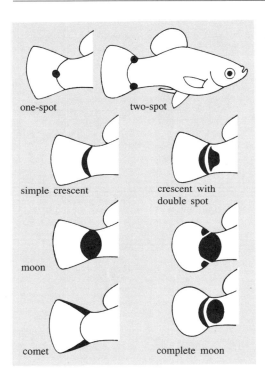

Platy markings. Shown here are the most common black markings of platys.

one-spot

two-spot

simple crescent

crescent with double spot

moon

comet

complete moon

female variatus platys grow to a length of 2³/₈ inches (6 cm).

Fin shapes: The only fin variation from the normal shape is a tall dorsal fin. In both males and females this fin is sail-like and, especially in males, a vivid yellow.

Ground and cover colors: Surprisingly, the only ground color found so far in variatus platys is the wild color. There are no albino or golden forms. The cover colors are blue, yellow, marigold (a yellowish orange), and black.

The most important and most common color combinations are as follows:

Sunset platys: Both sexes are bluish on the sides of the body, with yellow dorsal fin and red tail fin.

Hawaii platys: The entire body except for the head is black (without shiny scales). The dorsal fin of the male is yellow; that of the female, paler. Both sexes have bright red tail fins.

Marigold platys: The back and dorsal fins are yellow; the belly, lower half of the body, and the tail fin, orange (not red).

My Tip: By crossing platys and swordtails, almost any color combination can be achieved. However, I strongly discourage beginners from experimenting. It takes a lot of experience to end up with a pure strain from the genetic mishmash that results from crossings. With a little experience, however, almost any breeder can establish his or her own particular strain.

Tips for Selective Breeding of Platys

The same tips described for swordtails (see page 50) apply also to breeding maculatus and variatus platys. Male platys, though, are not as bellicose toward each other as male swordtails; and because platys are smaller, they can be kept in smaller tanks.

The Molly

There are two basic types of mollies: those with small dorsal fins and those with big ones. The size of the fin depends on which of the two *Poecilia* species the strain originated from: *P. sphenops* (small fins) or *P. latipinna* (large fins). At this point almost all the mollies available from pet stores are a mixture of these two types. Both the females and the males grow to about 3¹/₈ inches (8 cm). The dorsal fin is tall but not as big as the fins of the latipinna type.

Other fin shapes: Apart from these "normal" mollies, mollies with veil-like fins have been bred.

Well-known Ornamental Varieties

Ten Tips for the Selective Breeding of Mollies

1. Ornamental mollies that are imported often develop a higher than average rate of tuberculosis (see page 38). Be especially careful, therefore, to select healthy fish when you buy breeding stock.

2. Breeding tanks need a minimum capacity of 20 gallons (80 L). For *latipinna*-type mollies, 50-gallon (200-L) tanks are required.

3. Good lighting is important (see page 20) so that algae will grow. Algae are the favorite food of mollies.

4. The water temperature for breeding should be about 79°F (26°C).

5. Since mollies very rarely prey on their young, they can be bred in a species tank.

6. If you want the offspring to be healthy, you must maintain excellent water quality (see page 23).

7. Before attempting to create new varieties by crossing different strains, you must be sure your breeding stock is genetically pure.

8. If your tap water is soft and you have sailfin mollies (*Poecilia velifera*), you should add a little salt to the tank water.

9. Male mollies of the *latipinna* type need large tanks for their large dorsal fins to develop properly.

10. Mollies grow very slowly. Be patient!

In adult mollies of this kind, however, the fins are so long that the fish can hardly swim. More common are the lyre-tail mollies, in which all the fins except the tail fin are about twice the ordinary size, with the anterior or outer rays much elongated. In the tail only the uppermost and lowermost rays are elongated, giving the tail a forked shape. If the fins are veil-like or lyre-shaped, the gonopodium of the male is excessively long, and this sometimes results in an inability to fertilize the female. Fin shape is carried by a dominant gene. Thus you can obtain large-finned offspring by mating a normal-finned male with a large-finned female.

Colors: The best-known color is black; this fish is the so-called black molly. *Poecilia sphenops* with black spots had long been observed in the wild, although they are rather rare. It was not until the 1930s, however, that the first pure black *P. sphenops* were bred in the United States. From there they were introduced into Europe. Until about 1970 almost all black mollies sold were of the small-finned type, but they have been largely supplanted by fish that are the result of crossing small-

and large-finned strains. Very occasionally one sees black mollies of the latipinna type, the so-called midnight mollies. Their dorsal fin is set off in red.

Particularly among the sailfin mollies (*P. velifera*), albinos occur with some frequency, even if the breeding stock used is wild-colored, that is, green.

One recent novelty is the white molly. This variety is a shimmery silver-white. An even more recent introduction is the golden molly, which is golden yellow or marbled yellow and black.

Mollies of any color but black also occur as piebalds. They have small black dots distributed irregularly all over the body.

A special color variety of the *P. sphenops* type is the liberty molly. The males are blue on the sides and have red on the outside edges of the tail and dorsal fins. The colors, especially those of the fins, are fainter in the females. The liberty molly was developed by selectively breeding wild fish exhibiting similar colors.

Popular Live-bearers and Their Care

In the following pages you will find descriptions of some of the most important and popular live-bearers along with precise instructions on how to care for them. In my selection from among the approximately 250 species I have concentrated on those that are carried at least occasionally by dealers. The recommendations for keeping and breeding these fish derive mostly from my many years of experience as an aquarist.

Notes on the Instructions for Care

The descriptions are organized into four sections, one for each of the following fish families:
• Poeciliidae (live-bearing toothed carps)
• Goodeidae (Mexican topminnows)
• Hemirhamphidae (live-bearing halfbeaks)
• Anablepidae (four-eyed fish)

Name: The Latin name is always given; and if there is a commonly used English name, it is indicated as well. Within the family, the descriptions are listed in alphabetical order by the Latin name.

Appearance: The species is briefly described.

Size: The measurements given reflect the size reached in the wild. Many fish grow larger in an aquarium because they live longer under human care than they do in nature. If the size reached in nature differs significantly, this fact is noted.

Biotope: If known, the favored biotope within the area of the species's distribution is given. This information should help the hobbyist supply an appropriate and natural environment for the fish.

Tank: The minimum tank capacity for keeping the fish for their full lifespan is specified. Juvenile fish can, of course, be kept in smaller tanks but must then be moved to larger ones when they reach maturity.

Stratum: Here the tank area where the fish spend most of their time is indicated. The fish will now and then move into other areas, for example, when they are being fed.

Bottom = on the bottom or slightly above

Middle = in the largest section of the tank

Top = near the water surface

Water: The water properties indicated have in practice shown good results.

Setup: Suggestions are given for setting up the tank; also some comments on the habits of the species.

Tip on communities: Other fish species that are suitable tank companions for live-bearers are identified.

Food: Food appropriate for the species is mentioned, as well as favorite foods.

Sexual differences: The most important differences between the sexes are described.

Courtship behavior: Suggestions are given on what to watch for when the fish get ready to mate.

Breeding: Indicated here are the type of tank to use if you wish your fish to produce offspring, the behavior of the parent fish toward their young, the number of young per brood, and suitable rearing foods. The size of the brood is meant only to give you a general idea; the actual number varies a great deal and depends, among other factors, on the maintenance and breeding conditions. If there is no other indication, the water properties given under the heading "Water" apply also for breeding.

Special remarks: Here some special facts concerning the species are given, and other species requiring similar care are mentioned.

Live-bearing Toothed Carps Poeciliidae Family

Alfaro cultratus

Appearance: A very slender, pikelike fish with shiny bluish scales and steel-blue eyes. Size: Males up to 2¾ inches (7 cm); females up to 3½ inches (9 cm). Biotope: Moving water, preferably with vegetation, in northern Central America (Costa Rica to Panama). Tank: At least 20 gallons (80 L). Stratum: Top. Water: pH 7–8; 5–20°dH; 75–82°F

Popular Live-bearers and Their Care

(24–28°C). Setup: Tank with circulation and floating plants. Active species. Tip on communities: Small to medium-sized Central American cichlids. Food: Flies and mosquito larvae, small fish, supplemented with dry food. Sexual differences: Males smaller, with gonopodium. Courtship behavior: The male pursues the female for some time (parallel swimming) before mating. Breeding: Place female in a densely planted tank holding about 5 gallons (20 L) or more. If well supplied with live food, the parents do not prey on the young. From 20 to 40 young in a brood. Rearing food: *Artemia* nauplii. Special remarks: *A. huberi* has prettier colors but is seldom offered for sale.

Belonesox belizanus
Pike Live-bearer or Pike-top Minnow

Photo on page 63.

Appearance: Pikelike fish having a cylindrical body and a large mouth with clearly visible teeth. Grayish brown. Size: Males up to 4³/4 inches (12 cm); females up to 10 inches (25 cm). Biotope: Moving water, among dense vegetation, from southern Mexico to Nicaragua near the Atlantic Coast. Has recently been released in coastal areas of Florida. Tank: At least 40 gallons (160 L). Stratum: Top. Water: pH 6–8; 12–30°dH; 75–79°F (24–26°C). Setup: Shallow tank with dense vegetation, including floating plants. Tip on communities: Large, peaceful fish, such as loaches or catfish. Food: Live fish; give the young water fleas and mosquito larvae as long as possible. If they refuse to eat these, give them live fish. Sexual differences: Males smaller, with gonopodium. Courtship behavior: Not very elaborate. The males hide and lie in wait for females. Copulation is very brief since the females tend to eat the males. Breeding: Easy if the fish are well fed. Place the female in a small tank holding about 12¹/2 gallons (50 L) shortly before she is due (see page 42). For a few hours after giving birth an inhibition mechanism prevents the female from eating, so that the young are safe from her. Return the female to the maintenance tank as quickly as possible. From 15 to 20 young in a brood. Rearing food: water fleas and mosquito larvae; later, young guppies. Special remarks: Not a fish for beginners. If you don't have an adequate source of food fish, you should not buy or keep this species.

Brachyrhaphis episcopi

Appearance: A sturdily built fish with many red and black markings. Size: Males up to 2 inches (5 cm); females up to 2³/8 inches (6 cm). Biotope: Stagnant or slow moving, densely vegetated water in Central America (Panama and Costa Rica). Tank: At least 12 gallons (50 L). Stratum: Middle. Water: pH 7–8; 5–20°dH; 74–82°F (24–28°C). Setup: Dense cushions of hornwort at the water surface, open areas for swimming below; some planted corners at the bottom. Tip on communities: Armored catfishes, small cichlids. Food: Live food, especially mosquito larvae; alternate with dry food. Sexual differences: Males slimmer, with gonopodium. Courtship behavior: Not very elaborate. Breeding: In a densely planted species tank; if well fed, the parents will not prey on the young. From 10 to 20 young in a brood. Rearing food: *Artemia* nauplii. Special remarks: In recent years other species with even prettier colors have been imported, among them *B. roseni*.

Gambusia affinis and *G. holbrooki*
Mosquito Fish and Holbrook's Gambusia

Appearance: Plain, usually gray fish. Females resemble guppies; males are slender. Sometimes male *G. holbrooki* are spotted with black. Size: Male up to 1¹/8 inches (3 cm); females up to 2³/8 inches (6 cm). Biotope: Prefer stagnant waters of all kinds. Original distribution: *G. affinis*, southeastern United States; *G. holbrooki*, southwestern United States. Have been released since the turn of the century on all continents to control mosquitoes.

Popular Live-bearers and Their Care

Also found in southern Europe. Can easily be kept in a garden pool during the warmer part of the year. Strata: Middle, top. Water: pH 6–8; 5–30°dH; 68–79°F (20–26°C). Setup: Well-planted tank; unfussy species. Food: Mosquito larvae are the favorite food, but the fish also eat all other kinds (see page 42). Courtship behavior: Males pursue females often and take advantage of any opportunity to mate. Breeding: Pregnant females must be placed in a net (see page 40) or a densely planted tank because the adult fish hunt the fry. From 10 to 30 young in a brood. Rearing food: *Artemia* nauplii. Special remarks: Male *G. holbrooki* are quite often spotted with black. Some authorities regard these two kinds of mosquito fish as subspecies, *G. affinis affinis* and *G. affinis holbrooki*. Most other members of the *Gambusia* genus are sold only rarely and have similar requirements.

Girardinus falcatus
Yellow Belly

Appearance: Elongated, yellowish fish almost as transparent as glass. The young have blue eyes. Size: Males up to 2 inches (5 cm); females up to $2^3/4$ inches (7 cm). Biotope: Occurs only on Cuba; found there in the most varied biotopes but seems to prefer heavily vegetated waters. Tank: A species tank holding at least $7^1/2$ gallons (30 L) or a community tank of at least 15 gallons (60 L). Stratum: Middle. Water: pH 6.5–7.8; 5–20°dH; 75–79°F (24–26°C). Setup: Plant back of tank thickly, but leave plenty of space for swimming. Tip on communities: Small rainbow fishes, guppies, platys, armored catfishes. Food: Dry food and occasionally some water fleas and *Artemia* nauplii. Sexual differences: Males are smaller, with long gonopodium. Courtship behavior: The male follows the female with lowered gonopodium, then darts at her quickly, trying to impregnate her. Breeding: Presents no problem in a species tank because the adult fish rarely go after the fry. They may be able to distinguish their own young from other fry by their blue eyes. From 15 to 30 young in a brood. Rearing food: Dry food in small morsels, *Artemia* nauplii. Special remarks: Be careful when transferring fish from one tank to another. This species is sometimes very sensitive to abrupt changes in water conditions.

Girardinus metallicus
Metallic Live-bearer

Appearance: Elongated, pikelike body; sides have a metallic sheen; blue eyes. Size: Males up to $2^3/8$ inches (6 cm); females up to $3^1/2$ inches (9 cm). Biotope: Stagnant and not very fast-moving waters of all kinds on Cuba. Tank: At least $12^1/2$ gallons (50 L). Stratum: Middle. Water: pH 6–8; 5–20°dH; 75–79°F (24–26°C). Setup: Tank with planted sections that serve as shelters and resting areas; easy fish to keep if good water quality is maintained. Tip on communities: Other peaceful live-bearers, also armored catfishes. Food: Omnivorous. Sexual differences: Males almost a third shorter than females, with gonopodium. Courtship behavior: Males watch, preferably from a hiding place, for an opportunity to attack and impregnate a female. Breeding: Isolate females before they give birth; they produce young approximately every 28–30 days. Adult fish rarely go after the young, whose eyes are unmistakably blue. From 10 to 40 young in a brood. Rearing food: Crushed vegetarian flakes and *Artemia* nauplii. Special remarks: There is a variant in which the male has a black abdomen. Both sexes of this black-bellied version are somewhat smaller than those in the normal one, and the courtship behavior is more conspicuous.

Heterandria bimaculata

Appearance: Strong, spindle-shaped body; sides often have a yellowish sheen. Size: Males up to $3^1/8$ inches (8 cm); females up to 6 inches (15 cm). Biotope: Largish bodies of stagnant water and all kinds of not very fast moving water in Mexico and the Central American countries bordering on Mex-

Popular Live-bearers and Their Care

ico. Tank: Species tank of at least 25 gallons (100 L) or community tank of 50 gallons (200 L) or more. Stratum: Middle. Water: pH 6–8; 5–20°dH; 75–86°F (24–30°C). Setup: Large tank with plenty of open area for swimming; shoaling fish. Tip on communities: Large nonpredatory cichlids. Food: Omnivorous but eat primarily live food, including fry—and juveniles up to half their own size—of their own and of other species; females are especially voracious. Sexual differences: Males smaller and slimmer, with gonopodium. Courtship behavior: Males fight so fiercely that usually only one adult male survives. Courtship and mating are not accompanied by violence or special displays. Breeding: In a species tank with densely planted areas; adult fish prey on the fry. It is best to isolate pregnant females in densely planted tanks of about 5 gallons (20 L). From 20 to 80 young in a brood. Rearing food: Small morsels of dry food, water fleas.

Heterandria formosa
Midget Live-bearer or Mosquito Fish

Appearance: Lower half of body black; light beige above; females stocky, males slender. Size: Males up to ³/₄ inch (2 cm); females up to 1³/₈ inches (3.5 cm). Biotope: Shore areas of stagnant or slowly moving water, usually in heavy vegetation. In Florida and bordering states in the southeastern United States. Tank: Species tank of 2¹/₂ gallons (10 L) or more, or community tank of at least 15 gallons (60 L). Strata: Middle, top. Water: pH 6–8; 15–20°dH; 72–79°F (22–26°C). Setup: Tank with some areas of dense plants, but make sure there is plenty of room for swimming. Tip on communities: Small, peaceful fish, such as small characins and dwarf cichlids (*Apistogramma*). Food: Omnivorous (small food morsels). Sexual differences: Males smaller, with gonopodium. Courtship behavior: Males appear to "fence," using their gonopodia as sabers, but no injuries occur. Breeding: In a breeding tank with lots of floating plants, such as *Riccia*. A birth period, during which 1 to 5 young are born daily,

can last up to 4 weeks. The parent fish rarely go after the fry. From 5 to 30 young per birth period. Rearing food: Dry food, *Artemia* nauplii. Special remarks: These fish can be kept in a garden pool during the summer.

Limia melanogaster
Black-bellied Limia

Appearance: Elongated fish, sides of body bluish black; females sturdy. Size: Males up to 2 inches (5 cm); females up to 2³/₈ inches (6 cm). Biotope: All kinds of waters on Jamaica. Tank: At least 10 gallons (40 L). Stratum: Middle. Water: pH 6–8.5; up to 20°dH; 75–79°F (24–26°C). Setup: Densely planted tank with some space for swimming. Tip on communities: Other live-bearers, as well as characins, catfishes, and dwarf cichlids. Food: Omnivorous. Sexual differences: Males with gonopodium; females with large gravid spot. Courtship behavior: Males pursue females persistently; make sure, therefore, that there are hiding places among plants. Breeding: In a species or a breeding tank of at least 5 gallons (20 L). Adult fish do not go after the young. From 20 to 50 young in a brood. Rearing food: Dry food in small morsels; *Artemia* nauplii. Special remarks: Two similar species, *L. dominicensis* and *L. vittata*, have the same requirements. The females of *L. vittata* grow larger than those of *L. melanogaster*.

Limia nigrofasciata
Hump-backed or Black-barred Limia

Appearance: Very deep-bodied; ground color yellow with blackish blue transverse stripes. Size: Both sexes up to 2³/₄ inches (7 cm). Biotope: On Haiti in Lake Miragoane and nearby waters. Tank: Species tank of at least 20 gallons (80 L) or community tank of 25 gallons (100 L) or more. Stratum: Middle. Water: pH 6.5–7.5; 5–20°dH; 75–79°F (24–26°C). Setup: Partially planted tank with plenty of open swimming area; these fish need a lot of fresh water. Tip on communities: Placid

Popular Live-bearers and Their Care

fish, such as armored catfishes. Food: Omnivorous; need small live food every so often. Sexual differences: Males slimmer, more deep-bodied (especially as they grow older), with gonopodium. Courtship behavior: Males pursue females for a long period, trying constantly to mate. Breeding: In a species or a breeding tank of at least 10 gallons (40 L). Adult fish don't go after the young. From 10 to 40 young in a brood. Rearing food: Small live food. Special remarks: A similar species, *L. perugiae*, is more demanding in terms of water quality (low nitrate concentration) but otherwise has the same requirements.

Phallichthys amates
Merry Widow

Photo on page 46

Appearance: Deep-bodied, slender fish with yellowish body and white rims on the fins; blue eyes. Size: Males up to 1½ inches (4 cm); females up to 2⅜ inches (6 cm). Biotope: Moving, but not too fast water in the Atlantic watershed of Guatemala and Honduras. Tank: Species tank of at least 10 gallons (40 L). Stratum: Middle. Water: pH 6.5–7.5; 5–25°dH; 75–79°F (24–26°C). Setup: A few plants; frequent water changes; problem-free species. Tip on communities: Peaceful small fishes, such as neon tetras. Food: Omnivorous. Sexual differences: Males slimmer, with gonopodium. Courtship behavior: Males pursue females for some time before mating but don't harrass them too much. Breeding: Easy; use a species or breeding tank of at least 5 gallons (20 L). Adult fish don't go after the young. From 20 to 40 young in a brood. Rearing food: *Artemia* nauplii, small morsels of dry food. Special remarks: *P. pittieri* grows somewhat larger and is just as easy to keep.

Phalloceros caudimaculatus
Caudo or One-spot Live-bearer

Appearance: Stocky, spindle-shaped live-bearer with beige ground color. The original form

has a light-rimmed brown spot on the middle of the body, but often the entire fish is covered with black dots and patches. Size: Males up to 1½ inches (4 cm); females up to 2⅜ inches (6 cm). Biotope: Cool mountain streams and pools in southeastern Brazil, Uruguay, Paraguay, and northern Argentina. Tank: Species tank of at least 7½ gallons (30 L). Strata: Middle, top. Water: pH 6–7.5; 3–20°dH; 64–72°F (18–22°C). Setup: Create a few plant thickets in the tank; it is important to keep the water cool by adding plenty of fresh water. Food: Omnivorous. Sexual differences: Males are smaller and slimmer, with gonopodium. Courtship behavior: Not very noticeable. Males pounce on females unexpectedly. Breeding: Presents no problems if fish are kept in cool water; use a species or breeding tank holding at least 7½ gallons (30 L). Adult fish rarely pursue the fry. From 5 to 30 young in a brood. Rearing food: *Artemia* nauplii. Special remarks: In addition to the normal form there is a mottled species, the spotted live-bearer (*P. reticulatus*), and a variety called golden one-spot (*P. reticulatus auratus*). The spotted variety is kept fairly commonly and is a suitable fish for a garden pool in the summer.

Poecilia reticulata
Guppy

Photos on front cover, inside front cover, pages 63 and 64, and back cover.

Appearance: Elongated fish. Females are big; males, slender. Females are lead gray; males, all kinds of colors. Size: Males up to 1⅛ inches (3 cm); females up to 2⅜ inches (6 cm). Biotope: Stagnant and slowly moving water. Originally from southeast South America and some Caribbean islands; has been introduced into tropical waters all over the world to control mosquitoes. Is found in some warm streams in central Europe and even in Germany and the Netherlands. Tank: At least 5 gallons (20 L). Strata: Middle, top. Water: pH 5.5–8.5; 15–40°dH; 75–79°F (24–26°C). Can also adjust to pure lake

Popular Live-bearers and Their Care

water! Setup: Plant tank densely, leaving a little room for swimming; very easy fish to keep. Tip on communities: Small fishes, such as armored catfishes, platys, characins. Varieties with large fins are best kept by themselves. Food: Omnivorous; offer live food once a week. Sexual differences: Males smaller and more colorful, with gonopodium. Courtship behavior: Before mating, the male performs a lovely dance in front of the female, body curved in C-shape and fins spread wide. Breeding: Very easy. Maintenance or breeding tank of at least 5 gallons (20 L). Only young males and females seem to go after the fry and juveniles (because they have not yet learned not to?). From 10 to 40 young in a brood. Rearing food: Dry food. Special remarks: There are many different ornamental varieties. Unlike males of these cultivated varieties, males of the wild form display very little variation in fin and tail shape. The males of some wild strains have very pretty colors. The females are almost always a uniform lead gray. *Polcilia branneri* and *P. picta* are similar species but are much more demanding and therefore not recommended for beginners. Successful breeding, in particular, presents problems.

Poecilia sphenops
Pointed-mouth Molly or Black Molly

Photo on page 17

Appearance: Males are pike-shaped; females, plumper. Fins are often red or yellow; the body is blue. Size: Males 2³/₈ to 3¹/₈ inches (6 to 8 cm), rarely up to 4 inches (10 cm); females 2³/₄ to 4 inches (7 to 10 cm), sometimes considerably larger—supposedly up to and even over 8 inches (20 cm). Biotope: Wild form found in fresh and brackish water from Texas to Colombia —especially in rivers of Central America. Tank: At least 20 gallons (80 L). Strata: Middle, top. Water: pH 6.5–8; 20–30°dH; 75–82°F (24–28°C). Setup: Robust plants; floating plants for protection of the fry. Frequent water changes needed. Original

strain undemanding, but the ornamental black variety often susceptible to disease. Food: Omnivorous; algae are the favorite food of mollies. Sexual difference: Males smaller, with gonopodium. Courtship behavior: Males fight to establish a rank hierarchy. The weaker ones tend to be sickly, and only the alpha animal displays beautiful coloring. The courtship display itself is not conspicuous: the male swims along behind the female and tries to impregnate her. Breeding: Easy, in a maintenance tank. Adult fish don't go after the young. Males smaller than 2 inches (5 cm) should not be used for breeding. From 5 to 20 young in a brood. Rearing food: Dry food, algae. Special remarks: *P. mexicana* and *P. butleri* (see photo on page 17) are similar and have the same requirements.

Poecilia velifera
Sailfin Molly

Photo on inside back cover

Appearance: Sturdy, deep-bodied fish. Sides green with dark dots; often available as albinos (flesh-colored with red eyes). Size: In aquariums, males up to 4 inches (10 cm), females up to 6 inches (15 cm); as much as 2 inches (5 cm) bigger in the wild. Biotope: Bodies of water near the coast on the Yucatan Peninsula. Tank: At least 40 gallons (160 L). Strata: Middle, top. Water: pH 7.5–8; 25–35°dH; 77–82°F (25–28°C). Setup: Tank with large swimming area; otherwise tank-bred male offspring will not develop the tall fins typical of their species. Imported fish, in particular, need to have a bit of salt—¹/₅ ounce per quart (5 g per liter) of water—added to the tank at first, but this can gradually be discontinued. After acclimation this fish is suitable for a community aquarium. Food: Omnivorous; likes especially to eat algae. Can also be given vegetarian dry food. Sexual differences: Males with a tall, sail-like dorsal fin; gonopodium. Courtship behavior: Place either one male in a tank

Popular Live-bearers and Their Care

of at least 25 gallons (100 L) or several males in a tank of at least 50 gallons (200 L); otherwise there may be fighting during courtship. The displays are very conspicuous. The males try to impress the females by raising their dorsal fins high. Breeding: Not easy because the juveniles need sufficiently large tanks, at least 40 gallons (160 L), to grow up in. Adult fish hardly pursue the young. From 20 to 200 young in a brood. Rearing food: Vegetarian dry food, *Artemia* nauplii. Special remarks: *P. latipinna* is similar but rarely available and tends to be rather sickly in an aquarium.

Poeciliopsis gracilis
Porthole Live-bearer

Photo on page 17

Appearance: Elongated, slender fish with a row of 4 to 10 eye-sized black spots on the sides against the silvery ground color of the body. Fry have bluish eyes. Size: Males 1½ inches (4 cm); females 2¾ inches (7 cm). Biotope: Shore areas of stagnant and moving water along the Pacific and Atlantic coasts of southern Mexico to Honduras. The fish seek out thick algae and dense plant growth where available. Tank: At least 10 gallons (40 L). Strata: Middle, top. Water: pH 6–7.5; medium hard to hard (from about 6°dH); 77–82°F (25–28°C). Setup: Easy fish to keep. Replace about one-quarter of the tank water with fresh water every three weeks. Tip on communities: Other small live-bearers, such as *Heterandria formosa*; also dwarf cichlids (*Apistogramma*) and *Corydoras* catfishes. Food: Small live food, dry food (but not dry food exclusively). Sexual differences: Males smaller, slimmer, with very long gonopodium. Courtship behavior: Inconspicuous. The male approaches the female from behind and tries to pounce on her to mate. Breeding: Easy if fish are well fed. At one-month intervals up to 50 young are produced. Adult fish rarely go after them. Rearing food: *Artemia* nauplii, small morsels of dry food.

Xenophallus umbratilis
Swordtail

Appearance: Slender fish, yellowish brown. Size: Males up to 1½ inches (4 cm); females up to 2⅜ inches (6 cm). Biotope: Coastal waters with heavily vegetated sections in Costa Rica. Tank: At least 12½ gallons (50 L). Stratum: Middle. Water: pH 6.5–7.5; 5–20°dH; 75–79°F (24–26°C). Setup: Tank with some dense stands of plants but also open space for swimming. Frequent water changes. Easy fish to keep. Tip on communities: Preferably smaller species. Food: Omnivorous; offer small live food (*Artemia* nauplii) at least once a week. Sexual differences: Males have long gonopodium that is forked at the tip. Courtship behavior: Inconspicuous. Breeding: Not always problem-free because the young are sometimes quite sickly. Breed in species tank. Adult fish rarely go after the young. From 5 to 20 young in a brood. Rearing food: Small live food.

Xiphophorus helleri
Swordtail

Photos on pages 18, 63, 64

Appearance: Elongated body; ornamental varieties in many colors. Wild form, green with red lateral line. Size: Males up to 4¾ inches (12 cm) not including sword; females up to 5½ inches (14 cm). Biotope: Found in not too small bodies of water of all kinds, but generally prefers moving water. Occurs in the Atlantic watershed from Mexico to Belize. Tank: At least 20 gallons (80 L). Stratum: Middle. Water: pH 6–8; 10–30°dH; 75–79°F (24–26°C). Setup: Tank with circulation. Males aggressive toward each other and sometimes

Live-bearing toothed carps. Above, left: Ornamental guppy variety (*Poecilia reticulata*) with "bottom sword." Above, right: Wild form of the platy (*Xiphophorus maculatus*). Middle: Pike live-bearer (*Belonesox belizanus*). Below, left: Swordtail (*Xiphophorus nezahualcoyotl*). Below, right: Cortez swordtail (*Xiphophorus cortezi*).

Popular Live-bearers and Their Care

toward other species. Keep either a single male or several so that the aggression is dissipated among them. Food: Vegetarian, food animals, and food flakes. Sexual differences: Males are smaller and slimmer, with "sword" on the caudal fin; gonopodium. Courtship behavior: Males sometimes fight so fiercely that only the strongest survive. During actual courtship the male dances around the female in large sweeps and with widely spread fins. Breeding: Easy in a species or breeding tank of at least 12½ gallons (50 L). Adult fish occasionally go after the fry, and the female should therefore be isolated (net method, see page 41) before the brood is due. From 30 to 100 young in a brood. Rearing food: Dry food or small live food in small morsels. Special remarks: Many ornamental varieties. Wild strains also exist in many color variations and are occasionally available from dealers. *Xiphophorus cortezi* (see photo on page 63), *X. montezumae*, *X. nezhual coyotl* (see photo on page 63), and the dwarf species *X. nigrensis* and *X. pygmaeus* are similar but don't grow as large and are a little harder to take care of (give them a lot of fresh water!).

Xiphophorus maculatus
Platy

Photo on page 63

Appearance: Very deep-bodied, stocky-looking live-bearer. Females are gray; males, gray or black, occasionally with some red. Size: Males up to 2 inches (5 cm); females up to 2⅜ inches (6 cm). Biotope: Moving lowland water on the Atlantic side in the central section of Central America. Tank: At least 10 gallons (40 L). Stratum: Middle.

Live-bearing toothed carps. Above: In this ornamental variety of the guppy (*Poecilia reticulata*) the cover colors constitute an especially ornate design. Below: An ornamental swordtail variety (*Xiphophorus helleri*) with exceptionally long fins.

Water: pH 7–8; 12–30°dH; 75–79°F (24–26°C). Setup: Loosely planted tank, floating plants at the top to provide retreats for the fry. Tip on communities: Other live-bearers, such as guppies; labyrinth fish; armored catfishes. Food: All kinds of food that come in smallish morsels, especially vegetarian. Sexual differences: Males are smaller, with gonopodium. Courtship behavior: Inconspicuous. Breeding: Easy. Isolate pregnant females. Adult fish rarely go after the fry. From 10 to 50 young in a brood. Rearing food: Small morsels of dry or live food. Special remarks: Many ornamental varieties. The wild form also displays many color variations, depending on the river system from which the fish originally came. *Xiphophorus andersi* and *X. milleri* are similar species but are not as attractively colored.

Xiphophorus variatus
Sunset or Variegated Platy

Photos on page 28 and on back cover

Appearance: Elongated and slimmer than "normal" platys. Wild form has yellowish gray or blue sides. Biotope: Flat river sections with little current in southern Mexico. Tank: At least 12 gallons (50 L). Strata: Middle, top. Water: pH 6–8; 12–30°dH; 68–75°F (20–24°C). Setup: Tank with some areas of dense plants and open space for swimming. Good water maintenance important; otherwise the fish quickly deteriorate. This species cleans up the algae in the tank. Tip on communities: Other live-bearers, such as guppies; labyrinth fish; armored catfishes. Food: Vegetarian, also small live and nonvegetarian dry food. Sexual differences: Males slimmer, with gonopodium. Courtship behavior: The male tries to impress the female by spreading his fins wide in front of her. Breeding: Easy. Isolate pregnant females; raise young in a breeding tank of at least 7½ gallons (30 L). Adult fish rarely go after the fry. The young grow slowly. From 20 to 50 young in a brood. Rearing food: Small morsels of

Popular Live-bearers and Their Care

dry and live food. Special remarks: The colors vary with the river system from which the fish came.

Mexican Topminnows
Goodeidae Family

Ameca splendens

Photo on page 46

Appearance: Elongated, robust fish, anterior part of the body almost rectangular; long peduncle. Females silver-gray with dark spots; males green. Size: Males up to 3⅛ inches (8 cm); females up to 4 inches (10 cm). Biotope: Clear rivers with rocky sections and abundant vegetation in the area of the Rio Ameca in Mexico. Tank: At least 20 gallons (80 L). Stratum: Middle. Water: pH 6.5–8; 5–30°dH; 75–79°F (24–26°C). Setup: Tank with good circulation and plenty of swimming area. Peaceful species. Tip on communities: Other Central American live-bearers. Food: Omnivorous species but likes lots of vegetarian food, such as scalded spinach leaves. Sexual differences: Males smaller, yellow rim on caudal fin; andropodium. Courtship behavior: The male swims around the female with widely spread fins. Males may fight fiercly, but the loser usually emerges unharmed. Breeding: Very easy. Adult fish don't go after the big fry. From 5 to 30 young in a brood. Rearing food: Vegetarian dry food and small crustaceans. Special remarks: The females look very slender after giving birth to a brood. This is common in Goodeidae, and normally the females fill out again within a few days.

Characodon lateralis

Appearance: Stocky, cylindrical body. Females greenish; males with shades of red and yellow. Size: Males up to 2⅜ inches (6 cm); females up to 2¾ inches (7 cm). Biotope: Stagnant water in

northern Mexico in the vicinity of Durango. Tank: At least 12½ gallons (50 L). Stratum: Bottom. Water: pH 6–8; 5–20°dH; 75–79°F (24–26°C). Setup: Tank arranged in dark colors; this species requires a lot of fresh water and is not suitable for a community tank. Food: Omnivorous. Sexual differences: Males much more colorful than females, with shades of red; andropodium. Female greenish with spots on sides. Courtship behavior: The male tries to impress the female and maneuver her into mating position by displaying his widely spread fins. The female expresses her willingness to mate by shaking herself. Breeding: Not altogether easy. Only a few young are produced at a time. Use a species or breeding tank of at least 10 gallons (40 L). Adult fish don't prey much on the fry. From 3 to 20 young in a brood. Rearing food: Small live food. Special remarks: This is perhaps the loveliest member of the Goodeidae family.

Ilyodon furcidens

Appearance: Exceptionally elongated, slender live-bearer; yellowish green with violet areas on body. Size: Males up to 3⅛ inches (8 cm); females up to 4 inches (10 cm). Biotope: Generally in slow- to fast-moving rivers in the Pacific watershed along the edge of the Mexican Plateau. Tank: Species tank of at least 15 gallons (60 L) or community tank of 25 gallons (100 L) or more. Strata: Middle, bottom. Water: pH 6–8; 5–25°dH; 72–79°F (22–26°C). Setup: Robust plants, such as Java moss (these fish eat plants). Build shelters out of rocks. Tip on communities: Medium-sized fishes, such as characins and labyrinth fish. Food: Omnivorous, but prefers algae or scalded spinach leaves. Sexual differences: Males slender, with andropodium. Courtship behavior: Less conspicuous than in most other Mexican topminnows. Breeding: Easy. Use a species or a breeding tank of at least 10 gallons (40 L). Adult fish don't go after the fry. From 3 to 30 young in a brood. Rearing food:

Dry food, algae. Special remarks: Sometimes dealers label this species as *I. xantusi*.

Skiffia bilineata

Appearance: High-backed fish with large fins; grayish blue. Size: Males up to 1½ inches (4 cm); females up to 2¾ inches (7 cm). Biotope: Stagnant water in the central plateau of Mexico. Tank: At least 15 gallons (60 L). Stratum: Middle. Water: pH 6.5–8; 5–50°dH; 64–75°F (18–24°C). Setup: Tank with some thick stands of plants and lots of space for swimming. This fish reacts badly to abrupt water changes. Not suitable for a community tank. Food: Omnivorous but should get small live food twice a week. Sexual differences: Males have larger dorsal fin and are slimmer, with andropodium. Females are occasionally steel-blue. Courtship behavior: The male parades in front of the female with widely spread fins. The female shakes herself if she accepts his advances. Breeding: Not difficult in a species tank because the adult fish hardly go after the fry. From 3 to 20 young in a brood. Rearing food: Small live food. Special remarks: Not a fish for beginners!

Xenotoca eiseni

Photo on page 46

Appearance: Very high-back fish with the anterior part of the body being almost square. Ground color beige to gray. Males have orange peduncle and are occasionally golden yellow on the sides. Size: Males up to 2⅜ inches (6 cm); females up to 2¾ inches (7 cm). Biotope: Slowly moving as well as stagnant water along the southwestern slope of the Mexican plateau. Tank: At least 15 gallons (60 L). Stratum: Middle. Water: pH 6–8; 5–20°dH; 75–79°F (24–26°C). Setup: Robust plants, such as Java moss (this fish eats plants). Build shelters out of rocks. Tip on communities: Preferably no fish with long fins. Food: Omnivorous; offer plenty of live food before the fish breed. Sexual differences: Males more colorful, with andropodium. Courtship behavior: Exceptionally conspicuous: the male shows off his widely spread fins before the female, and she shakes if she responds positively to his advances. Breeding: Easy. Isolate pregnant females. Adult fish rarely go after the fry. Females older than 1½ years no longer produce young. From 3 to 30 young in a brood. Rearing food: Dry and live food in small morsels. Special remarks: This species exists in several variations with somewhat different colors.

Live-bearing Halfbeaks
Hemirhamphidae Family

Dermogenys pusillus
Wrestling or Malayan Halfbeak

Photo on page 26

Appearance: Long, very thin fish; silver-gray to bronze in color, with red edges on fins. Size: Males up to 2 inches (5 cm); females up to 2¾ inches (7 cm). Biotope: Shallow areas of not very fast moving rivers of all kinds in Southeast Asia. Tank: At least 15 gallons (60 L). Stratum: Top. Water: pH 5.5–8; 2–20°dH; 79–86°F (26–30°C). Setup: Tank with light circulation; plants that reach to the water surface and some floating plants. Can be kept in a brackish-water aquarium; add ⅓ ounce (10 g) of salt per 1 quart (1 L) of water. Tip on communities: Peaceful fish that live in the middle and bottom strata. Food: Insects, mosquito larvae; also dry food. Sexual differences: Males are smaller and more colorful, with andropodium. Courtship behavior: Males fight so violently that generally only one survives even in very large tanks. The actual courtship is not very conspicuous. Breeding: Difficult. Isolate females before they are due to give birth. From 5 to 30 young in a brood. Rearing food:

Popular Live-bearers and Their Care

The best way is to give the fry a teaspoon of chopped tubifex, springtails, or *Artemia* nauplii per feeding. Special remarks: A number of varieties of this species are sold. Another species, *D. ebrardtii*, is sometimes imported, too. It resembles the halfbeaks of the *Nomorhamphus* genus (see page 69) in body shape and in requirements for maintenance and breeding.

Hemirhamphodon pogonognathus

Appearance: Even longer and thinner than *Dermogenys pusillus*; bluish body. Size: Both sexes grow to about 4 inches (10 cm). Biotope: In rivers of the entire Malayan Peninsula. Tank: At least 25 gallons (100 L). Stratum: Top. Water: pH 5–8; 2–20°dH; 79–86°F (26–30°C). Setup: Tank with light circulation; plants that reach to the surface of the water and some floating plants. Avoid abrupt changes in water conditions; fish are negatively affected by poor water quality. Food: Insects, mosquito larvae. Sexual differences: Males are slimmer, with andropodium. Courtship behavior: Males don't fight as violently as those in other species of this family. The actual courtship is not very conspicuous. Breeding: Very difficult; has thus far hardly ever been accomplished. In a species or breeding tank of at least 7 ½ gallons (30 L). Isolate females before they are due to give birth. During the birthing period 1 to 4 young are produced daily. From 3 to 20 young in a brood. Rearing food: The best way is to give the fry a teaspoon of chopped tubifex, springtails, or *Artemia* nauplii per feeding.

Nomorhamphus liemi liemi and *N. liemi snijdersi*

Photo on page 26

Appearance: Noticeably more compact than the halfbeaks previously described. Ground color beige. Fins have a lot of red and black on them.

Size: Males up to 2 inches (5 cm); females up to 4 inches (10 cm). Biotope: Cool mountain streams in Sulawesi (Indonesia) as high as 3,200 feet (1,000 m) and more above sea level. Tank: At least 20 gallons (80 L). Stratum: Top. Water: pH 6–7; 2–20°dH; 68–75°F (20–24°C). Setup: Strong circulation. Floating plants. Frequent water changes important. Tip on communities: Peaceful, not too small fish that live in middle and bottom strata. Food: Fry and small crustaceans. Sexual differences: Males much smaller and more colorful than females, with protruding black lower jaw; andropodium. Courtship behavior: Males fight so persistently that only one survives. The actual courtship is not very conspicuous. Breeding: Relatively easy if the females are fed a good diet. Spawning tank with a dense cover of floating plants to provide hiding places for the fry, which are ¾ inch (2 cm) long. Adult fish prey on the fry, so raise the young in a rearing tank. From 3 to 10 young in a brood. Rearing food: *Artemia* nauplii and other live food. Special remarks: The two subspecies differ only slightly from each other. The markings on the fins of *N. liemi snijdersi* are almost always black only, without red. Occasionally other species of this genus are sold. They have the same requirements for maintenance and breeding as the species described here.

Four-eyed Fish
Anablepidae Family

Anableps anableps
Four-eyed fish

Photo on page 45

Appearance: Long, cigar-shaped body, beige to gray. Size: Males up to 8 inches (20 cm); females up to 12 inches (30 cm). Biotope: Slowly moving rivers extending to salt water; fish most commonly found in brackish water. Widely distributed in Central America and the coastal areas of northeastern South America. Tank: At least 65 gallons (250 L). Stratum: Top. Water: pH 6.5–8.5; 10–50°dH; 75–79°F (24–26°C). Setup: Difficult fish to keep. Large, shallow tank with 8 inches (20 cm) of water and no plants; use rocks to provide hiding places. Brackish water. Acclimate gently, adding ⅓ ounce (10 g) of salt per 1 quart (1 L) of water; later you can try to shift very gradually to fresh water. Food: Dry food flakes, mealworms, flies. Sexual differences: Males slender, with tubelike gonopodium. Court-

ship behavior: Not conspicuous. The male approaches the female from behind and stimulates her by pushing against her repeatedly before mating. Breeding: In a species tank; difficult. Only females in excellent condition produce young. Adult fish prey on the fry. From 1 to 10 young in a brood. Rearing food: Small live food. Special remarks: Because a band of tissue divides the eyes into two parts, this species is able to see above and below water simultaneously. Be careful; these fish are excellent jumpers!

Useful Literature and Addresses

Books

Hansen, J.: *Making Your Own Aquarium* (Bell and Hyman, 1979).
Hawkins, A.D. (editor): *Aquarium Systems* (Academic Press, 1981).
Ramshorst, J.D. van (editor): *The Complete Aquarium Encyclo*...
Scheurmann, Ines: *Aq*...
ron's, 1990).
————: *The New Aqu*...
1986).
————: *Water Plants*...
1987).
Stadelmann, Peter: *Tro*...
Sterba, G.: *The Aquar*...
ford, 1983).
Ward, Brian: *Aquari*...
(Barron's, 1985).

Magazines

Aquarium Fish Magaz...
P.O. Box 6050
Mission Viejo, CA 92...

Freshwater and Marine Aquarium
144 West Sierra Madre Boulevard
Sierra Madre, CA 91024

Practical Fishkeeping Magazine
RR1, Box 200D
Jonesburg, MO 63351

...es

...ialty Societies

...sociation

...y Association

...eders Guild

Index

Index